FACES OF RACISM

are to be ret

FACES OF RACISM

● ● ●

Josef Szwarc

AMNESTY
INTERNATIONAL

Faces of Racism
Josef Szwarc

August 2001
© Amnesty International UK
99-119 Rosebery Avenue
London EC1R 4RE

Faces of Racism is the first in an introductory series
on key human rights issues.

The views expressed in this book do not necessarily reflect the
views of Amnesty International.

Cover: *Montage of pictures featured throughout the book.*
Bottom left: John Muafangejo detail from Bishop RH Mize etc
© *John Muafangejo Foundation*

ISBN 1 873328 55 9
AIUK product code PB250

Introduction

Among my girlfriends, among our friends, in our family, there are Serbs and Croats and Muslims. It's a mixed group and I never knew who was a Serb, a Croat or a Muslim. Now politics has started meddling around. It has put an 'S' on Serbs, an 'M' on Muslims and a 'C' on Croats, it wants to separate them. And to do so it has chosen the worst, blackest pencil of all – the pencil of war which spells only misery and death.

Entry in the diary of 11 year-old Zlata Filipović, 19 November 1992, a resident of Sarajevo, Bosnia-Herzegovina, which was besieged and bombed during a civil war between ethnic groups in the former Yugoslavia.[1]

Most of the family I should have known were murdered before I was born. Looking at their photographs, hearing about their destruction and dispersal, was my introduction to the world of 'us' and 'them'. The world in which our fate is determined by the group in which we happen to be born, rather than our actions or innate potential.

Race and racism
In this book 'race' is used as an umbrella term for various population groups of which people think themselves to be members, or to which

The lynching of Rubin Stacy, 19 July 1935, Fort Lauderdale, Florida.

they think other people belong. Thus, 'black',* 'white', 'Jew', 'Roma'* and so forth are described as racial groups, because people identify them as such. These identities affect how people treat and are treated by people of other groups. Race includes groups distinguished by skin colour and appearance and what are commonly called ethnic groups, that is people with shared cultural, linguistic and historical backgrounds.

This approach to defining race has been described as a 'social' one because it is concerned with how people perceive the world and how those perceptions affect their conduct. It does not purport to describe biologically distinct groups. Race is real because people believe it to be important, regardless of scientific arguments. In the words of biologist Dr Eric Lander, 'there's no scientific evidence to support substantial differences between groups'.[2]

'Racism' is used in this book to describe:

- negative attitudes towards or beliefs about a group because they are of a different race or
- discrimination against people because of their race.

Faces of Racism also describes negative attitudes and discrimination towards people on the grounds that they have come from another country. Like people victimised because of their race, 'foreigners' are targeted by a circumstance of their birth, not on account of what they believe or what they have done.

The definition of racism in this book follows the definition of racial discrimination in the 1996 international treaty, the Convention on the Elimination of All Forms of Racial Discrimination, which prohibits discrimination on the basis of race, colour, descent, ethnic and national origin.

National anti-racist laws and anti-racist organisations also adopt a broad definition of the groups that they aim to protect. In their mid-1980s study of immigrants in Western Europe, Castles, Booth and Wallace noted that in Continental Europe 'racism' had historically been used to apply mainly to anti-semitism and the treatment of indigenous peoples in the colonies, but was increasingly used to refer to discrimination against the 'new ethnic minorities' including Italians, Yugoslavs and Turks. They observed:

Choice of terminology is not neutral: it implies a political perspective. Continental anti-racists speak of racism to emphasise that the treatment of foreign residents has much in common with past treatment of Jews or subjugated people.[3]

About the book

Faces of Racism seeks to illuminate the nature of racism by describing both the ideas of advocates and the deeds of perpetrators. The topics are arranged alphabetically with an entry for each letter from A to Z but do not constitute a comprehensive account of the subject.

Within each of the topics, the examples are intended to illustrate that racism is universal and that in various forms it has appeared throughout history. As Peter Gay notes:

The Hebrews of the Old Testament believed that Abraham's covenant with the Lord set them apart from lesser mortals. The Egyptians of the Old Kingdom took their fertile land as proof that the creator-god Ra had singled them out in preference to the miserable Asians. The Greeks thought themselves better than the barbarians... The animus was always the same... the more one loved one's own, the more one was entitled to hate the Other.[4]

The topics and the illustrations are also intended to reflect that racism is pervasive, affecting how people behave in their personal relationships and in their public roles as employers, jurors, police officers and politicians. Researchers have found that 'racial prejudice is common not only in adults and adolescents but also in children,' and that children as young as five show high levels of prejudice.[5]

Psychologists, sociologists, historians and scholars in other disciplines have sought to understand the sources of racist attitudes and behaviour in individuals and societies. The literature is vast and there is no comprehensive explanation of the diverse forms in which racism arises, flourishes and subsides. (Some particular texts of interest are cited in Sources, page 122).

I find compelling the analysis of Albert Memmi, who suggests that racism is 'inherent in the human condition':

[E]ach time one finds oneself in contact with an individual or group that is different and only poorly understood, one can react in a way that would signify a racism... Are we then all racist for all times? No, not exactly. But we are all tempted by racism, yes. There is in us a soil prepared to receive and germinate its seeds the minute we let down our guard. We risk behaving in a racist manner each time we believe ourselves threatened in our privileges, in our well being, or in our security.[6]

Faces of Racism describes laws that prohibit racism and the sources provide information about anti-racist resources and organisations. Laws and other measures are important but I believe they will fail without a further critical element: the courage of individuals. Visiting South Africa during the era of apartheid, US politician Robert Kennedy observed that 'it is from the numberless diverse acts of courage and belief that human history is shaped. Each time a person stands up for an ideal, or strikes against injustice, he sends forth a tiny ripple of hope; and crossing each other from a million different centers of energy and daring, those ripples build a current which can sweep down the mightiest walls of oppression'.[7]

This book mentions a small number of people who have confronted racism at grave personal risk, but it is not only life and death situations that demand such strength. It takes courage to tell a relative, a friend or work colleague that their conduct is wrong. It takes courage to stand by the stranger who is being insulted. It takes courage for politicians to forego the votes they might obtain by pandering to the electors' fears and prejudices. It takes courage to examine one's own attitudes and actions.

Josef Szwarc, London, August 2001

---

*NOTE:
The book uses the terms and spelling – including capitalisation – of racial groups that are generally used in the UK. Where there is no common UK term, the book uses the name and spelling that is used internationally [for example, in United Nations documents] or in the relevant country.
The term 'Gypsies', commonly used for Roma people, is now widely considered derogatory.

Apartheid

The school must equip the Bantu to meet the demands which the economic life of South Africa will impose on him...There is no place for him in the European community above the level of certain forms of labour... Until now he has been subject to a school system which drew him away from his own community and misled him by showing the green pastures of European society in which he is not allowed to graze... What is the use of teaching a Bantu child mathematics when it cannot use it in practice?

South African Education Minister [and later Prime Minister] Hendrik Verwoerd addressing Parliament, June 1954.[1]

● ● ●

Only white people live or work in the South African town of Orania and that is how the residents want it to remain. In 2000, the town asked the government to recognise it as a whites-only 'homeland', with power over local matters. 'This is all about self-sufficiency, not racism,' town official Roelien de Klerk explained. 'We don't hate blacks, we just don't want to rely on them anymore.'[2]

The township is overlooked by a statue of former Prime Minister Verwoerd, one of the leading advocates and architects of the system of white domination known as 'apartheid' that was imposed in 1948. It means 'separateness' or 'apartness' in Afrikaans.

Apartheid greatly extended the scope and intensity of racially discriminatory measures that had been introduced in South Africa

From a coastal street at Strand, near Cape Town, a black worker passes a sign reminding him that only white people could use this stretch of beach for recreation.

© Corbis Image

throughout the 20th century. People were formally classified as white, Bantu [black], Coloured [mixed race] or Asian. Rights of residence, employment, political participation and other matters were determined on the basis of these classifications. More than 80 per cent of the land was set aside for the white population, though there were approximately five times as many black people. Black South Africans required passes to be in 'non-black' areas and were not entitled to vote. Miscegenation – inter-racial marriage – was prohibited.

All sectors of society were drawn into an elaborate and brutal system, as acknowledged by Craig Williamson, a former key member of internal security services:

Our weapons, ammunition, uniforms, vehicles, radios, and other equipment were all developed and provided by industry. Our finances and banking were done by bankers who even gave us covert credit cards for covert operations. Our chaplains prayed for our victory, and our universities educated us in war. Our propaganda was carried by the media, and our political masters were voted back in power time after time with ever-increasing majorities.[3]

In 1973, the member states of the United Nations adopted the International Convention on the Suppression and Punishment of the Crime of Apartheid, declaring that acts intended to establish and maintain domination by people of one racial group over people of another violate international law. Another 20 years of domestic and international pressure were required before South Africa's apartheid rulers conceded defeat. In 1994 people of all races elected the first government with a black majority and a black President, Nelson Mandela.

Official racial discrimination in other countries

Apartheid was introduced in South Africa just three years after the defeat of Nazi Germany, which had also established a comprehensive framework of racial discrimination, in this case mainly against Jews and Roma. Though the war was hailed as a victory over a brutal racist regime, some of the countries that defeated Germany themselves had racially discriminatory laws and policies that continued for many years after the war. In the USA, for example, a number of states had laws segregating public facilities such as education, transport and leisure, and laws prohibiting miscegenation. Aboriginal Australians were subject to officially sanctioned discrimination, such as unequal rates of pay, and denial of the right to vote.

Despite the adoption of international treaties prohibiting racial discrimination in the 1960s and 1970s, significant gaps remained between rhetoric and practice. These are just two examples:

Israel: Since the nation's foundation in 1948, state-owned land

● An armed Fijian rebel leads a group of coup supporters in the capital Suva on 27 May 2000. Indigenous Fijian rebels held the Prime Minister and members of his multi-racial government hostage for 56 days, demanding that ethnic Indians be permanently stripped of political power.

(comprising more than 90 per cent of the country's total) was allocated exclusively to Jews. This resulted in the denial of housing opportunities to Israeli Arabs. One affected couple was Adel and Iman Qadan, who were refused the right to buy a home in the town of Katzir because they were Arabs. The Qadans petitioned the courts and in March 2000 Israel's Supreme Court ruled that the policy of refusing land to Israeli Arabs was illegal.[4]

Malaysia: Malaysian law distinguishes between *bumiputeras* –

literally 'sons of the soil' – who are defined as ethnic Malays and other indigenous peoples and non-*bumiputeras*, by far the largest group of whom are ethnic Chinese (about 27 per cent of the population). *Bumiputeras* are entitled to 'special rights' and this has been the basis of a system of political, educational and economic discrimination favouring mainly Malays.[5]

De facto segregation

'Apartheid' is now commonly used to describe not only racial segregation that is officially sanctioned but also the *de facto* social, economic and residential segregation along racial lines that is apparent in many countries. To those who perpetrate and benefit from segregation, and those who are its victims, the difference between legislated and de facto segregation may be insignificant.

In the Great Lakes Region of Africa – Rwanda, Democratic Republic of Congo and Burundi – the Batwa Pygmy people are subject to extreme segregation by neighbouring groups. 'Other people will not eat or drink with them, will not marry them, will not allow Batwa to approach too close, to sit with them on the same bench or touch cooking and eating implements.'[6]

In Brazil, racial discrimination is prohibited by law. However, when United Nations racism expert Mr Glèlè-Ahanhanzo visited the country in 1995, he found that discrimination was 'an ordinary feature of life'.[7] In employment, for example, there was virtually a 'racial division of labour'. White people dominated senior level positions in both public administration and private enterprises; the vast majority of black women were domestic workers, nursemaids or samba dancers in night-clubs.

The expansion of the term apartheid to include de facto segregation is mirrored in the expansion of the meaning of 'ghetto'. The ghetto was originally a section of Venice where Jews were compelled to live following an edict of the Catholic Church in 1179, forbidding Jews and Christians from living together. Today it is the poor area of any city where the socially and economically disadvantaged are concentrated, trapped by poverty and prejudice rather than obliged by law. It is no coincidence that in many countries high proportions of people in the ghetto are from racial minorities.

See also: **Caste, Porraimos**

B

• •

Biology
Science, race and racism

... it's a trade off: more brain or more penis. You can't have everything.

Canadian psychologist Professor J Phillipe Rushton, a leading proponent of the view that there are innate differences between racial groups in traits such as intelligence, 1986.[1]

● ● ●

Are racial differences superficial or significant? Is colour of skin and shape of nose related to intelligence, creativity, criminality, laziness, morality and athleticism? Over the centuries, people have given quite different answers to these questions. Their answers have profound social, economic and political consequences.

In the mid-18th century, Scottish philosopher David Hume wrote: *I am apt to suspect Negroes to be naturally inferior to the Whites. There scarcely ever was a civilised nation of that complexion, nor ever any individual, eminent either in action or speculation. No ingenious manufactures among them, no arts, no sciences. On the other hand, the most rude and barbarous of all the Whites, such as the ancient Germans, the present Tartars, have still something eminent about them in their valour, form of government, or some other particular. Such a uniform and constant difference could not happen, in so many countries and ages, if nature had not made an original distribution between these breeds of men...*[2]

In the 19th century, the size and shape of skulls, the weight and configuration of brains and features of other parts of the body became important subjects of study for a number of scientists and pseudo scientists seeking to understand and explain racial differences. US doctor Samuel George Morton theorised that brain size correlated with intelligence. Morton measured the size of hundreds of skulls and between 1839 and 1849 he published studies that showed significant differences in cranial capacity by race: 'Caucasian' groups were the biggest, followed by 'Mongolian', 'Malay', 'American' and 'Negro'.

Morton's data was reviewed in 1977 by Stephen Jay Gould who reported that Morton's methods and analysis were flawed. For example, Morton failed to take account of differences in the stature of the groups whom he studied: 'Morton used an all-female sample of three Hottentots to support the stupidity of blacks, and an all-male sample of Englishmen to assert the superiority of whites.'[3] Morton's 'findings' were not deliberately falsified, Gould believes: '[a]ll I can discern is an *a priori* conviction about racial ranking so powerful that it directed his tabulations along pre-established lines.'[4]

Social scientists also expounded the view that there was a biologically determined racial hierarchy of talent. In his *Essay on the Inequality of Human Races* (1853), French anthropologist Joseph de Gobineau theorised that there were two important hierarchies, one of colour and one within the white races:

Human history is like an immense tapestry... The two most inferior varieties of the human species, the black and yellow races, are the crude foundation, the cotton and the wool, which the secondary families of the white race make supple by adding their silk; while the Aryan group, circling its finer threads through the noble generations, designs on its surface a dazzling masterpiece of arabesques in silk and gold.[5]

Consequences of scientific racism

Gobineau's ideas were a central element of the ideology of Nazism and of the genocidal policies of the German Nazi regime. The Aryan race, Adolf Hitler proclaimed, was 'the bearer of human cultural development' and the maintenance of Aryan purity and vigour were critical to the future of civilisation:

What we must fight for is to save the existence and reproduction of our race and our people, the sustenance of our children and the purity of our blood, the freedom and independence of the

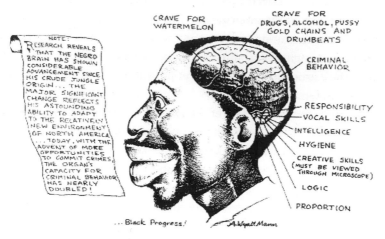

fatherland, so that our people may mature for the fulfilment of the mission allotted to it by the creator of the universe.[6]

Racial science imported into Africa by European missionaries, explorers and anthropologists in the 19th and early 20th centuries contributed to genocide on that continent as well. The Europeans theorised that Rwandan Tutsis were both racially distinct from and superior to the Hutus. 'The theory was based both on the appearance of many Tutsi – generally taller and thinner than were most Hutu – and European incredulity over the fact that Africans could, by themselves, create the sophisticated kingdom that the first white men to arrive in Rwanda found there.' A theory called the 'Hamitic hypothesis' was promulgated, suggesting that the Tutsi had sprung from a superior 'Caucasoid' race from the Nile Valley.[7]

The belief that the two groups were so distinct influenced the attitudes and conduct of both Europeans and of Tutsis and Hutus themselves, creating and intensifying divisions. During the genocidal confict of 1994, Tutsi victims were thrown into the Nyabarongo River, a tributary of the Nile, and told to 'meet their parents in Abyssinia' (former name of Ethiopia) – a reference to the Hamitic theory's account of their origins.'[8]

In the USA in the first half of the 20th century, psychologists who studied intelligence were the main scientific protagonists of racial hierarchy. Their research findings fuelled political concern about the 'quality' of immigrants entering the USA and in 1924 the *Immigration Restriction Act* was passed with the aim of cutting the number of people coming from southern and eastern European countries. It was 'one of the greatest victories of scientific racism in American history', Stephen Jay Gould has observed.[9]

Following the Second World War, scientists from around the world collaborated to provide a concise, public rebuttal of the intellectual basis of racism. Under the auspices of the United Nations, they produced a series of 'Statements'. The most recent, in 1967, says: *Racism falsely claims that there is a scientific basis for arranging groups hierarchically in terms of psychological and cultural characteristics that are immutable and innate. In this way it seeks to make existing differences appear inviolable as a means of permanently maintaining the current relations between groups.*[10]

Psychology continues to be the main field in which researchers assert that there are biologically determined racial differences. In 1994, US academics Richard J Herrnstein and Charles Murray published *The Bell Curve*, surveying a large number of studies that purportedly demonstrate that racial differences in intelligence are to a significant extent due to genetic – and therefore immutable – factors. Critics argued that there were serious flaws in the research methods of Herrnstein and Murray and of the authors whose work they relied upon.[11]

In 2001 scientists completed a study of the human genome sequence which found that 'humans are 99.9 per cent genetically identical'.[12] 'No serious scholar in this field now considers race to be a scientific concept,' says genetic researcher Dr Craig Venter.[13]

See also: **On the Origin of Species**

C
●　●

Caste

When we are working, they ask us not to come near them. At tea canteens, they have separate tea tumblers... We cannot enter temples. We cannot use upper-caste water taps. We have to go one kilometre away to get water... When we ask for our rights from the government, the municipality officials threaten to fire us. So we don't say anything. This is what happens to people who demand their rights.

A Dalit woman, Ahmedabad district, Gujarat State, India 1998[1]

●　●　●

In January 2001, millions of people gathered at Allahabad by the Ganges River for the Hindu festival of Kumbh Mela. In order to cope with the influx, the authorities erected a tent city with hospitals and police stations. For sanitation, a British journalist reported, 8,000 'turd-pickers' were employed. The term prompted a sharp response from reader Reverend David Haslam who pointed out: 'The cavalier reference to "8,000 turd-pickers"...masks a grimmer reality. They are some of the hundreds of thousands of Dalits (the old "untouchables") who are still designated the toilet cleaners of Indian society. Their health is poor, they are regarded as polluted and their "trade" is passed on from generation to generation.'[2]

'Dalit' means broken or oppressed people. It was adopted by Indian campaigners to describe members of the hereditary social group or caste that was formerly referred to as 'Untouchables'.

A demonstration led by a women's organisation outside Sarwar police station on 14 September 1999 protesting about abuses of the rights of a Dalit woman and family by police.

© Mahila Jan Adhikar Samiti

Untouchables were traditionally associated with occupations that Hinduism regarded as 'impure', in particular those involving contact with faeces and other emissions from the human body. Their touch was believed to pollute other castes and they were therefore subject to severe social and economic segregation. The discrimination affected every man, woman and child and, as noted above, was passed from generation to generation. 'They are bound to their fate at birth, escaping only at the time of their death,' in the words of Dalit activist R Eugene Culas.[3]

Mahatma Gandhi, Indian independence activist, sought to undo the stigma suffered by the Untouchables by calling them 'Harijans', meaning Children of God. Dalit human rights campaigners have

21

rejected the term: 'Today, this group refuses to be patronised as the object of sentimental piety. They emphasise their identity by calling themselves Dalits.'[4] It is estimated that perhaps 160 million people – a sixth of India's population – are Dalits.[5]

Discrimination against Dalits is illegal and the Indian government has instituted various programmes to promote Dalit welfare. However, Dalits continue to experience considerable discrimination, particularly in rural areas. The United Nations Committee on the Elimination of Racial Discrimination has expressed concern at reports that Dalits 'are often prevented from using public wells or from entering cafes or restaurants and that their children are sometimes separated from other children in schools'.[6]

Human rights organisations and others have reported that Dalits are often the victims of serious crimes against their persons and their property. After an extensive investigation of the Dalit situation in the state of Rajasthan during the 1990s, Indian journalist Paligummi Sainath reported that on average 'a dalit woman is raped every 60 hours. One dalit is murdered a little over every nine days... A dalit house or property suffers an arson attack every five days'.[7]

Victims do not complain because they fear retribution or lack faith in the police. Human Rights Watch reports that 'police refuse to register complaints about violations of the law and rarely prosecute those responsible for abuses that range from murder and rape to exploitative labor practices and forced displacement from Dalit lands and homes.'[8]

Landlords, employers and others whose power has been challenged by Dalit activists have retaliated, often brutally. 'Whenever the Dalits have tried to organise themselves or assert their rights,' an Indian government agency reported in 1998, 'there has been a backlash from feudal lords resulting in mass killings of the Dalits, gang rapes, looting and arson.'[9] Amnesty International has documented attacks on Dalit rights defenders and cites the following case as illustrative of its concerns:

In July 1998 a dalit *activist from Jalma district of Maharashtra was attacked and killed by upper caste members of his village when he returned in the middle of the night to visit his wife and new-born child. He had been banned from the district for two years after several criminal cases were registered against him by police (reportedly at the instigation of a local factory owner opposed to his activities in raising awareness amongst the* dalit *community of their*

*rights). He reportedly had his tongue cut out and his hands and legs
cut off before his body was set fire to.*[10]

The Indian government contends that the caste system is based on
social and economic distinctions not 'race'. However, the definition of
racial discrimination in the Convention on the Elimination of Racial
Discrimination includes discrimination on the basis of 'descent'. It
therefore covers caste, in the view of the United Nations committee
that monitors countries' compliance with the Convention.

Caste systems outside India

Long-established caste systems persist in other countries as well. In
Nepal, for example, 'so-called untouchables cannot even enter the
houses of the people of so-called higher and middle-class castes'.[11]

The untouchable people of Japan are the *Burakumin*, a word
derived from the Japanese for village or hamlet. The *Burakumin* are
descendants of people who were segregated residentially and
occupationally by law in the 17th century. They were assigned
occupations that Shinto and Buddhism considered 'polluting' such as
the slaughter of animals. *Burakumin* are pejoratively called *eta*,
meaning 'pollution abundant' or 'extreme filth'.

The Japanese government formally abolished *Burakumin* as a
distinct class in 1871. However, more than a million people who are
identified as *Burakumin* live in thousands of 'ghetto-like'
communities throughout the country and are discriminated against in
various areas of life. Private detectives are engaged by employers to
investigate whether job applicants are *Burakumin* and by parents to
check the background of their children's fiancés. During 2000, the
Buraku Liberation League – an organisation campaigning on behalf
of *Burakumin* people – received reports of hundreds of incidents of
discrimination, 'ranging from graffiti and anti-buraku websites to
abuse in the workplace'.[12]

See also: **Apartheid, Miscegenation**

23

'Driving While Black'

Institutional racism

**I'm so popular with the security guards at the Pick and Pay
[supermarket] that my criminal white friends have started using me
as a decoy.**

Black South African comedian Kagiso Lediga, 2001.[1]

● ● ●

The American Civil Liberties Union (ACLU), a US human rights
organisation, reports the 1997 case of Charles and Etta Carter, an
elderly African-American couple from Pennsylvania, who were
stopped by Maryland State Police on their 40th wedding anniversary:
*The troopers searched their car and brought in drug-sniffing dogs...
Their belongings were strewn along the highway, trampled and
urinated on by the dogs. No drugs were found and no ticket was
issued. The Carters eventually reached a settlement with the Maryland
State Police.*

The Carter case is one of many – 28 in 18 states in early 2001 – reported
by the ACLU as instances of police using race as a criterion to decide
which drivers to stop and search for illegal drugs.[2] Criminologists
describe the practice as 'racial profiling'. Black people refer to being
stopped for the unlegislated crime of 'Driving While Black'.
    US police began targeting black and Hispanic or Latino drivers in
the context of the so-called 'war on drugs' that greatly intensified
during the 1980s. In 1999 New Jersey State authorities established an

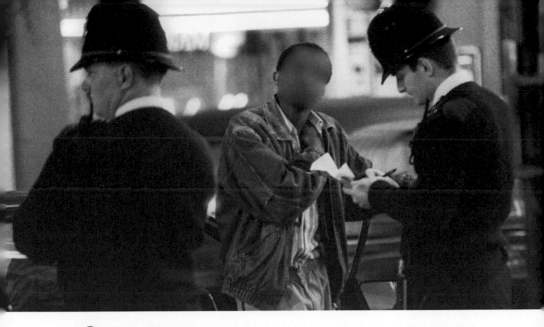

● In the UK, ethnic minorities – particularly black men – are stopped and searched by police in far higher proportion to their share of the overall population. The Stephen Lawrence Inquiry concluded that this reflected, in part, racist stereotyping.

© David Hoffman Photo Library

inquiry which concluded that despite explicit policies prohibiting racial profiling, 'the problem of disparate treatment is real not imagined'.[3] In two areas where police stopped motorists, eight out of 10 searches involved minority drivers. The inquiry concluded that while there was wilful misconduct by a small number of police, that was not the main cause of the discrimination:

[There were] more common instances of possible de facto discrimination by officers who may be influenced by stereotypes and may thus tend to treat minority motorists differently during the course of routine traffic stops, subjecting them more routinely to investigative tactics and techniques that are designed to ferret out illicit drugs and weapons.[4]

Racial discrimination has also been apparent in other criminal justice matters in the USA, including the application of the death penalty. In August 2000, death row prisoner Brian Roberson appealed to Texas Governor (now President) Bush to commute his execution because the prosecutor had deliberately excluded black people from the jury – in some US states with the death penalty, juries decide whether or not a convicted person should be executed. According to his lawyers, when

25

Roberson was convicted in the 1980s there was a pattern of racial discrimination in jury selection, evidenced by the following:

'If you ever put another nigger on a jury, you're fired'
– the reported remark of District Attorney Henry Wade to then-Assistant District Attorney Jack Wade after a jury hung because a black woman would not convict.

'Do not take Jews, Negroes, Dagos, Mexicans or a member of any minority race on a jury, no matter how rich or how well educated'
– advice on jury selection provided in guidelines prepared by Bill Alexander, aide to Henry Wade.

'Minority races almost always empathise with the Defendant.'
– advice in a jury selection manual used to train prosecutors until the early 1980s.[5]

Studies in a number of states in the USA have consistently shown that there is a significantly greater likelihood of the death penalty being imposed in cases where the victim is white or the defendant is black. More than 80 per cent of the 500 people executed between 1977 and 1999 were convicted for the murder of a white person, although black and white people are the victims of homicides in almost equal numbers.[6] 'Race is more likely to affect death sentencing than smoking affects the likelihood of dying from heart disease,' says the Death Penalty Information Center, a US research and advocacy organisation. However, the centre says that while evidence about the dangers of smoking 'has produced enormous changes in law and societal practice, racism in the death penalty has been largely ignored…'[7]

In the mid 1960s black American activists Stokely Carmichael and Charles V Hamilton coined the term 'institutional racism' to draw attention to covert, pervasive discrimination that was as deadly as the overt violence of racist individuals.

When white terrorists bomb a black church and kill five black children, that is an act of individual racism, widely deplored by most segments of the society. But when in that same city – Birmingham, Alabama – five hundred black babies die each year because of the lack of proper food, shelter and medical facilities, and thousands more are destroyed and maimed physically, emotionally and intellectually because of conditions of poverty and discrimination in the black community, that is a function of institutional racism.[8]

Analysts in other countries have adopted and adapted the concept to describe their circumstances.

In the UK, black youths Stephen Lawrence and Duwayne Brook were attacked by a group of white youths in 1993. Stephen Lawrence was fatally stabbed. No one was charged with his killing. Stephen Lawrence's parents complained that the manner in which the police handled the investigation was seriously flawed by racism and after a lengthy campaign the government established an inquiry.

The inquiry determined that racism had indeed been an important factor and concluded: 'Mere incompetence cannot of itself account for the whole catalogue of failures, mistakes, misjudgements, and lack of direction and control which bedevilled the [police investigation].'[9] The failure of the police was not due to overt discrimination by a few individuals who were hostile to black people, the inquiry report stated, but to 'pernicious and persistent institutional racism', which it defined as:

The collective failure of an organisation to provide an appropriate and professional service to people because of their colour, culture or ethnic origin. It can be seen or detected in processes, attitudes and behaviour which amount to discrimination through unwitting prejudice, ignorance, thoughtlessness and racist stereotyping which disadvantages minority ethnic people.[10]

The second sentence of the Lawrence inquiry's definition is significant because it confined 'institutional racism' to discrimination that occurs unconsciously or unintentionally. The influence of the inquiry's definition was apparent shortly afterwards when the head of Britain's prison service, Martin Narey, announced that there would be an inquiry into racism in prisons. Mr Narey reportedly acknowledged that the service was 'not only institutionally racist but that pockets of malicious racism exist'.[11] When they coined the term 'institutional racism', Stokely Carmichael and Charles Hamilton did not make such a distinction. In their view, the same racist attitudes underlie both individual and institutional racism:

Institutional racism relies on the active and pervasive operation of anti-black attitudes and practices. A sense of superior group position prevails: whites are 'better' than blacks; therefore blacks should be subordinated to whites. This is a racist attitude and it permeates the society, on both the individual and institutional level, covertly and overtly.[12]

Ethnic cleansing

There is no room for two distinct races of white men in America, much less for two distinct races of whites and blacks…We can never attain the ideal union our fathers dreamed, with millions of an alien, inferior race among us, whose assimilation is neither possible nor desirable… You and we are different races. We have between us a broader difference than exists between almost any other two races. Whether it is right or wrong I need not discuss, but this physical difference is a great disadvantage to us both, as I think your race suffer very greatly, many of them by living among us, while ours suffer from your presence. In a word we suffer on each side. If this be admitted, it affords a reason at least why we should be separated.

US President Abraham Lincoln at a ceremony for American blacks leaving to settle in Africa, 1862.[1]

In 1819 the US Congress authorised President Monroe to provide $100,000 to the American Colonization Society to purchase a location in Africa in which free blacks could be 'colonised', that is, settled. The Society purchased land in West Africa that became the colony of Liberia in 1822. In honour of President Monroe, the capital was named Monrovia.

When President Lincoln issued the 1862 Emancipation Proclamation

● West Kalimantan [Indonesian Borneo] 2001 – indigenous Dayak people attacking homes of people whom the Indonesian government moved to West Kalimantan from Madura in order to reduce that island's high population density. Dayaks opposed the migration programme because it has pushed them off their land and was seen as a means of 'civilising' the Dayaks. Hundreds of people, mainly Madurese, have been killed in recurrent outbreaks of violence.

© AFP

freeing all slaves in the USA, he made clear his preference that they would make use of their liberty by leaving. The declaration stated that 'the effort to colonize persons of African descent... will be continued'. The US government's policy was to accomplish separation by encouraging black people to return to Africa voluntarily. Despite the support of a number of black leaders relatively few people agreed to leave.

During the 20th century, politicians in other countries implemented or canvassed schemes to encourage people of unwanted races to depart voluntarily. However, the hallmark of the century is forcible expulsion, a phenomenon that came to be known as 'ethnic cleansing'. The term entered common use in the 1990s to describe events occurring in the former Yugoslavia.[2] Other incidents throughout the 20th century illustrate the term equally well.

Australia In 1901, the British colonies in Australia united and formed an independent country. The new nation's political leaders, with overwhelming public support, were agreed that Australia should

29

be racially white. One of the first measures of the national Parliament was legislation to expel Pacific Islanders who had been recruited – sometimes by force – to work on sugar plantations in the colony of Queensland.

The children of Pacific Islanders who were born in Australia were exempt from deportation and a group of 54 petitioned the Governor of Queensland to allow their parents to remain. They wrote: 'We appeal to you, that representations be made to the proper authorities, that separation of families may not take place, and that all our parents may be permitted to live in this country of our birth.' The authorities made some concessions but otherwise the programme of expulsion was implemented. Between 1904 and 1908 more than 7,000 people were deported.[3]

Uganda When Britain was forced to cede independence to its former East African colonies, it handed over only the reins of government. Considerable economic power remained in the hands of non-indigenous people and has been the focus of conflicts in which the very future of those people in Africa has been an issue.

In Uganda, for example, people of Asian origin were prominent in many areas of trade. Indigenous Africans resented their success and their social exclusiveness. This was exacerbated by the apparent lack of commitment by people of Asian origin to the country following independence, when many chose to retain British citizenship rather than to become Ugandan nationals.

In August 1972, Ugandan President Idi Amin declared that 'all Asians, citizens or not, must leave'. Amin's announcement unleashed a wave of anti-Asian violence by both officials and ordinary citizens. Tens of thousands of Ugandan Asians fled. Even in the course of making their escape many were victimised. Letters from a group who went to India 'told of being stopped on the way by bands of Ugandan soldiers, of all their belongings taken, of the men made to lie down on the ground while the women were raped'.[4]

Europe The scale and frequency of racially motivated expulsions in Europe in the 20th century far exceeded that of any other region of the world. In 1922, for example, Greece and Turkey agreed to exchange more than a million people. During the Second World War, Germany expelled a million Poles and Jews from western to eastern Poland and brought ethnic Germans into the region to take their place. When Germany was defeated, the victors expelled millions of ethnic Germans, both those who had settled recently and those of long-established communities.

In the 1990s, the federation of states comprising Yugoslavia began to fracture along ethnic lines. In the ensuing conflicts various parties sought to establish territories populated only by their own ethnic group. Their methods included murder, rape, torture, expulsions, destruction of places of worship and cutting off supplies of food to civilian population centres.[5] The conflicts were soon widely described as ethnic cleansing, which a United Nations expert team succinctly defined as 'rendering an area ethnically homogenous by using force or intimidation to remove persons of given groups from the area'.[6]

Governments and their officials have not been the sole perpetrators of ethnic cleansing. Private citizens as well have often been involved, sometimes acting in concert with the authorities and sometimes on their own initiative. In Kosovo, for instance, members of the ethnic Serb populace helped soldiers and militia to drive ethnic Albanians from the province until military intervention by NATO in 1999. Subsequently ethnic Albanians have forced Serbs to leave. Roma have been 'excluded or expelled from numerous municipalities throughout Europe', according to a recent study. 'In some instances, their exclusion has been effected through formal policy; in others, Roma have been expelled by lawless force.'[7]

Ethnic cleansing under international law

Although ethnic cleansing is not specifically named as a crime under international law, the conduct that it involves is clearly prohibited. The Nuremberg Tribunal tried Nazis following the Second World War for 'crimes against humanity' which were defined as including 'deportation, and other inhumane acts committed against any civilian population, before or during the war...'[8]

The Geneva Conventions cover crimes committed in the course of both international and civil wars. 'Individual or mass forcible transfers' are prohibited during international conflicts (Article 49 of the Fourth Geneva Convention). Combatants in civil wars are required to treat humanely those people who are not actively taking part in the hostilities, 'without any adverse distinction founded on race, color, religion or faith, birth or wealth'. (Article 3, common to the four Geneva Conventions)

Ethnic cleansing is also not cited as a crime that can be tried by the permanent International Criminal Court that is currently being

A group of Bosnian Moslems, refugees from Srebrenica, walk to be transported from the eastern Bosnian village of Potocari to Moslem-held Kladanj near Olovo (July 13, 1995). The United Nations issued a damning report on its actions leading up to the 1995 killings of Bosnian men in Srebrenica, blaming itself and the Security Council for failing to use force and appeasing the Serbs.

established. However, the crimes within its jurisdiction cover both direct acts of ethnic cleansing – such as the deportation of civilians – and acts that may be intended to force people to flee, such as rape.

See also: **Imperialism, Porraimos**

Faith

Religion and racism

[T]he holding of slaves is justifiable by the doctrine and example contained in the Holy Writ and is therefore consistent with Christian uprightness, both in sentiment and conduct.

A statement of the Baptists' position on slavery, forwarded to the Governor of South Carolina by the Reverend Dr Richard Furman, 1823.[1]

● ● ●

Religion has provided a basis both for racism and for opposition to racism. More accurately perhaps, we should speak of the people rather than their creeds. As UN Secretary-General Kofi Annan has observed about 'the dark side' of the practice of religion: 'Religion is not itself to blame… the problem is not usually with the faith, but with the faithful.'[2]

This section looks at the contrasting roles of religion in relation to imperialism, slavery and genocide. The examples involve primarily leaders and adherents of Christianity, but this is not to suggest that Christianity is more prone than other religions to inspire either racism or anti-racism.

Imperialism, slavery and their aftermath

In the 15th century, the Portuguese and Spanish rulers actively sought Papal approval for their brutal conquest of the Americas. Pope Nicholas V's response to these 'athletes and intrepid champions of the Christian faith' was generous and they were granted

free and ample faculty to invade, search out, capture, vanquish, and

● Adolf Hitler shakes hands with Lutheran Bishop Ludwig Muller, accompanied by Benedictine Abbot Alban Schchleiter. A number of German church leaders gave Christian support to the German nationalism of the Nazi party while others struggled to keep their religion out of politics.

subdue all Saracens [Muslims] and pagans whatsoever, and other enemies of Christ wheresoever placed, and the kingdoms, dukedoms, principalities, dominions, possessions, and all movable and immovable goods whatsoever held and possessed by them and to reduce their persons to perpetual slavery ...[3]

In North America as well, defenders and opponents of slavery used theological arguments. The main scriptural justification was the so-called 'curse of Ham', a son of Noah, in the Book of Genesis 9:25-27. Angered that Ham had seen him naked, Noah laid a curse upon Ham's son, Canaan, that Canaan and all his descendants would be slaves. Many Christians believed that Canaan settled in Africa, and identified black Africans as his descendants and therefore subject to the curse.

Others found Christianity a source of inspiration to oppose slavery. On a number of occasions, according to historian David Chidester, 'African Americans drew on Christian resources to inspire and mobilize revolts against slavery'.[4] Baptist preacher Nat Turner led an uprising in Virginia in 1831. He was captured and as he was taken to the gallows to be hanged he reportedly stated, 'Was not Christ crucified?'[5]

One hundred years after the abolition of slavery, Christianity continued to be a source of strength for black campaigners, as black civil rights activist Rosa Parks explains:

People often ask me, 'Why was the church a part of the movement?' It was the only legal place our people could gather and get information without being harassed or unjustly treated… The church was and is the foundation of our community. It became our strength, our refuge, and our haven. We would sing, pray, and meet in church. We would use Scriptures, testimonies, and hymns to strengthen us against all the hatred and violence going on around us.[6]

While her colleague Reverend Martin Luther King also acknowledged the importance of religion, he noted that the 'white church and its leadership' opposed racism but with few exceptions failed to actively support anti-racist campaigning. Imprisoned for his civil rights work in Birmingham Alabama, King wrote to religious leaders expressing his disappointment in their stance:

I felt that the white ministers, priests and rabbis of the South would be among our strongest allies. Instead, some have been outright opponents, refusing to understand the freedom movement and misrepresenting its leaders; all too many others have been more cautious than courageous and have remained silent behind the anesthetizing security of stained-glass windows.[7]

Genocide

In Europe during the 1930s and 1940s, the brutal racist programmes of Nazi Germany and its allies created stark distinctions between faith communities as agents, victims or opponents of oppression. The Nazis exploited the history of strong anti-Jewish prejudice in European Christianity and readily found both sympathisers and silent witnesses.

'God is on the side of the White Man...' Wilhelm Schultz in *Simplissimus* 3 May 1904

Some Catholic bishops openly stated anti-Semitic views. 'There will be the Jewish problem as long as the Jews remain,' Cardinal Hllond, Primate of Poland, observed in 1936.[8] Despite repeated calls both externally and from within the Catholic Church for Pope Pius XII to speak out, his response was a 'self-imposed silence', in the words of historian John Cornwell. The Pope's stance reflected his personal anti-

Semitism and his assessment of the strategic interests of the Church, Cornwell suggests, and amounted to 'complicity in the Final Solution through failure to register appropriate condemnation...'[9]

In contrast, Church leaders in a number of countries strongly criticised the persecution of the Jews and other groups. Metropolitan Stephan of Sophia – head of the Bulgarian Orthodox Church – publicly condemned attacks on Jews and Kiril, Bishop of Plovdiv, stated that if a plan to deport Jews proceeded he would personally lie across the railway tracks to block the first transport.[10]

Looking at the pattern of victimisation, historian Helen Fein found that 'the majority of Jews evaded deportation in every state occupied by or allied with Germany in which the head of the dominant church spoke out *publicly* against deportation before or as soon as it began... The greater the church resistance, the fewer Jews became victims'.[11]

The dual role of religion and of religious leaders was also apparent in the 1994 genocide in Rwanda. Cleavages between the Hutus and Tutsis were strengthened – if not created – by the 'pernicious doctrines' with which generations of schoolchildren were indoctrinated by Catholic missionaries, according to an inquiry.[12] When the genocide erupted, some priests and pastors actively assisted the perpetrators and senior church leaders were indirectly complicit by failing to denounce what was occurring. In June 2001, a Belgian court convicted two Catholic nuns charged with helping Hutu militias kill people fleeing the genocide.

On the other hand, hundreds of nuns, pastors and priests were prominent among the opponents of the genocide:

[They] hid the hunted and the vulnerable, tended the wounded, reassured the terrified, fed the hungry, took in abandoned children, confronted the authorities, and provided solace and comfort to the exhausted and the heart-broken.[13]

They did so knowing the risk: as many as one quarter of Rwanda's Catholic clergy and many other clerical people were killed.

See also: **Apartheid, Caste, Genocide, Imperialism, Slavery**

G
● ●

Genocide

...from the very first day they clapped eyes on them the Spanish fell
like ravening wolves upon the fold, or like tigers and savage lions
who have not eaten meat for days. The pattern established at the
outset has remained unchanged to this day, and the Spaniards still do
nothing save tear the natives to shreds, murder them and inflict upon
them untold misery, suffering and distress, tormenting, harrying and
persecuting them mercilessly... When the Spanish first journeyed
there, the indigenous population of Hispaniola [now Haiti and
Dominican Republic] stood at some three million; today only three
hundred survive. The island of Cuba... is now to all intents and
purposes uninhabited; and two other large, beautiful and fertile
islands, Puerto Rico and Jamaica, have been similarly devastated.

From an account prepared by Spanish missionary Bartolomé de Las Casas in the mid-
16th century.[1] A modern historian has described the destruction of the Indians of the
Americas as 'far and away, the most massive genocide in the history of the world'.[2]

● ● ●

Naming the crime
Those who committed the horrors reported by Bartolomé de Las
Casas did so without real fear of punishment. There was no justice
system – laws, investigators, prosecutors and courts – to hold them to
account. For the next four centuries, little changed. Entire groups of
people were destroyed in the course of imperialism and other conflicts
and the people responsible – those who fired the guns and the political

and military leaders who armed and directed them – were rarely if ever held to account.

The systematic murder and enslavement of civilians during the Second World War was, according to British Prime Minister Winston Churchill, 'a crime without a name' but one that the UK and its allies were determined should be punished. Before the war had ended the crime was to have a name – 'genocide' – suggested by international lawyer Raphael Lemkin, which he coined from the Greek *genos* – race or tribe - and the Latin *cide* – killing.[3]

In 1948 the member states of the United Nations agreed to adopt a treaty, the Convention on the Prevention and Punishment of the Crime of Genocide, that defined the crime and required governments to prevent and punish it. The Convention defines genocide as specified acts that are committed with the intention of destroying, in whole or in part, a national, 'ethnical', racial or religious group. The acts that are specified are

- Killing members of the group;
- Causing members of the group serious bodily or mental harm;
- Deliberately inflicting conditions of life calculated to physically destroy all or part of the group;
- Imposing measures intended to prevent births within the group;
- Forcibly transferring children of the group to another group.

Since 1948, two international tribunals have been established to try people charged with the crime of genocide. One deals with crimes committed in the former Yugoslavia after 1991. The other tribunal deals with events that occurred in Rwanda during 1994, when the country's Hutus killed perhaps as many as one million of their Tutsi fellow nationals. In 1998, Jean Kambanda, a former Prime Minister of Rwanda, became the first person convicted for the crime of genocide by an international court since the Genocide Convention was adopted.

Other modern genocides
Events that have occurred during the last fifty years in many countries other than the former Yugoslavia and Rwanda have been described as constituting the crime of genocide as defined by the Convention. They include the following.

Australia – The Stolen Generation From 1910 to 1970 between one in three and one in 10 Aboriginal children were forcibly removed

● Armenian Christians killed in Adana in the Ottoman Empire, 1909, one of a series of massacres committed by Turkish forces after 1895. More than a million Armenians may have perished in massacres and death marches beginning in 1915, which has been described by some as the first genocide of the 20th century.

© Mary Evans Picture Library

from their families and their communities and placed with white people. They came to be called 'the stolen generation'. The main objective of the policy of removing the children, according to the Australian Human Rights and Equal Opportunity Commission – an official human rights agency – was to assimilate them into the non-indigenous community 'so that their unique cultural values and ethnic identities would disappear'. This objective was genocidal, the Commission declared, 'because it aims to destroy the "cultural unit" which the [Genocide] Convention is concerned to preserve'.[4]

Brazil Concerned about reports of atrocities being committed against Indians by officials of the Indian Protection Service (SPI), the Brazilian Congress in 1967 commissioned an inquiry by attorney Jader Figueiredo. Figueiredo's 5000-page report documented mass murder, torture, slavery and sexual abuse. According to Figueriedo, the suffering of the Indians was similar to that experienced by people in Nazi concentration camps, and he concluded that 80 tribes had 'disappeared completely'.[5] The SPI had been 'a den of corruption and indiscriminate killings', Figuerido reported.[6] One hundred and thirty four officials were subsequently charged with more than 1,000 crimes against the Indians but no one was ever imprisoned.

Guatemala During a civil war between 1992 and 1996, according to a United Nations sponsored inquiry, the Guatemalan army systematically set out to destroy groups of Maya whom they considered were actual or potential supporters of the guerrillas.

The massacres, scorched earth operations, forced disappearances and executions of Mayan authorities, leaders and spiritual guides, were not only an attempt to destroy the social base of the guerrillas, but above all, to destroy the cultural values that ensured cohesion and collective action in Mayan communities.[7]

The inquiry concluded that the government's conduct constituted genocide within the meaning of the Genocide Convention.

Iraq The Iraqi government has been accused of genocidal conduct in relation to its Kurdish minority, who number about 4 million and have long campaigned for autonomy. In response to a Kurdish uprising, in 1987-88 the government implemented brutal measures, targeting civilians as well as Kurdish forces. According to Human Rights Watch, the campaign was characterised by

mass summary executions and disappearances of many tens of thousands of non-combatants; the widespread use of chemical weapons, among them mustard gas and nerve agents that killed thousands; and the wholesale destruction of some two thousand villages along with their schools, mosques, farms, and power stations.[8]

See also: **Ethnic cleansing, Faith, Imperialism, On the Origin of Species, Porraimos, ZOG**

41

In 1975-1979, a group called the Khmer Rouge ruthlessly imposed radical political, economic and cultural policies on Cambodia. Perhaps 2 million people were murdered or died as a consequence of Khmer Rouge measures. The Khmer Rouge attack on the population is often referred to as genocide though some commentators say it does not fit the legal definition in the Genocide Convention because in the main Khmers were killing Khmers.[9]

Hate speech

Inge sits in the reception room of the Jew doctor. She has to wait a long time. She looks through the journals which are on the table. But she is much too nervous to read even a few sentences. Again and again she remembers the talk with her mother. And again and again, her mind reflects on the warnings of her leader of the League of German Girls. 'A German must not consult a Jew doctor. And particularly not a German girl. Many a girl went to a Jew doctor to be cured, found disease and disgrace!'

Extract from *The Poisonous Fungus*, a German children's book, written by Ernst Hiemer and published by Julius Streicher in 1938.[1]

● ● ●

Julius Streicher was a key author and disseminator of the anti-semitism that the Nazis exploited to come to power and implement a program of genocide. Adolf Hitler understood well the importance of hate speech for his purposes: 'Anti-semitic propaganda in all countries is an almost indispensable medium in the extension of our political campaign.'[2] In power, the Nazi regime devoted significant resources to spreading anti-semitic ideas through books and journals, film and radio as well as speeches at rallies.

The scale of the Nazi propaganda machine has never been matched by any other racist group. But hatred can be spread by crude and simple means – by word of mouth, graffiti, posters and newspapers. The internet now offers racists a sophisticated medium

TWO FORCES.

John Tenniel's cartoon shows Britannia (Britain) protecting Hibernia (Ireland) from the forces of anarchy, represented by an apelike Irishman. The apelike image of the Irish was also used by US cartoonist Thomas Nast in *Harper's Weekly*.

© Punch

with which to reach a potentially massive audience inexpensively and anonymously.

Looking at instances of hate speech in different countries and in different times, several key themes recur, including:

Scapegoating: target groups are often alleged to be responsible for social, economic and other problems.

Non-human descriptions: racists commonly describe their target groups as animals or insects – *ratons* ['rats', French colonial settler reference to Algerians]; *bobbejaan* [baboon, South African Afrikaner reference to black Africans]; *guayaki* [rabid rats, Paraguayan settler reference to hunter-gather Ache people]; *inyenzi* [cockroach, Rwandan Hutu reference to Tutsi]. White football fans in the UK and Italy make monkey sounds to abuse black players from opposing teams. The implication of such references is clear: if the target group is not human, its members can be treated accordingly.

Criminality: one of the most pervasive themes of hate speech is the allegation that members of the target group are prone to commit crimes ranging from theft and fraud to murder. The Nazis fear of the Jew as sexual predator, illustrated in the children's story on page 43, resonates in white people's perceptions of black men in the USA and Serb perceptions of ethnic Albanians in Kosovo. For centuries, Roma in Europe have been seen as prone to crime.

Hate speech and freedom of expression

For his role as a Nazi propagandist, Julius Streicher was tried by the Nuremberg Tribunal. The prosecution's submission to the court was that Streicher bore a heavy responsibility because he had made the crimes committed by others possible.

In its extent [the prosecution concluded], Streicher's crime is probably greater and more far-reaching than that of any of the other defendants. The misery which they caused ceased with their capture. The effects of this man's crime, of the poison that he has put into the minds of millions of young boys and girls goes on... He leaves behind him a legacy of almost a whole people poisoned with hate, sadism, and murder, and perverted by him.[3]

Streicher was found guilty and executed. Nearly 50 years later, hate propaganda was again a catalyst of genocide. In 1994, broadcasters on Rwandan radio station Radio-Television Libre des Mille Collines called upon Hutus to kill and drive from the country Tutsis, Belgians and political opponents of the regime. One of the broadcasters, Georges Ruggui, was tried by the International Criminal Tribunal for Rwanda on a charge of incitement to commit genocide. He pleaded guilty and was sentenced to imprisonment for 12 years.[4]

Many governments considered that the lesson of Nazi Germany was that a balance had to be struck between freedom of expression and freedom from racism. This is reflected in, for example, the 1996 International Covenant on Civil and Political Rights which provides both that 'everyone shall have the right to freedom of expression' and that governments must prohibit the advocacy of racial hatred that incites discrimination, hostility and violence.

Individual countries have adopted quite varied approaches to

45

striking a balance between freedom of expression and suppressing racist speech.

The challenge of determining when it may be appropriate to restrict freedom of expression is demonstrated in a case that divided the Canadian Supreme Court. In 1984, James Keegstra was convicted of violating a criminal law prohibiting the wilful promotion of hatred against 'identifiable groups', for example people distinguished by colour, race or religion. Keegstra was a high school teacher who had taught that Jews sought to destroy Christianity and were responsible for wars and depressions. Keegstra appealed against his conviction, arguing that the offence infringed the guarantee of freedom of expression in the Canadian Charter of Rights and Freedoms.

By a bare majority – four to three – the Supreme Court held that the offence did not infringe the Charter. The court noted that the Charter stipulates that the rights are subject to reasonable limits that can be justified in a democratic society. Accordingly, the government might be justified in banning the propagation of ideas that are hostile to democratic values, such as advocating racial and religious discrimination. It was irresponsible, the majority held, for society to act on the assumption that if ideas were permitted to compete freely, truth would defeat falsehood. 'We know that under strain and pressure in times of irritation and frustration, the individual is swayed and even swept away by hysterical, emotional appeals.'[5]

US law is significantly more protective of freedom of speech. The US Constitution prohibits laws 'abridging the freedom of speech' without a qualification such as that in the Canadian Charter of Rights and Freedoms.

In 1977-8, the National Socialist Party of America (NSPA) – described by its leader as a Nazi Party – announced plans to march in the village of Skokie, Illinois. It selected Skokie for the demonstration because the village had a large Jewish population. Village authorities passed ordinances to prohibit the march and the dissemination of material that promoted or would incite racial or religious hatred. The NSPA successfully challenged the ordinances as an unlawful restriction on its constitutional right to freedom of expression. 'Above all else,' the court stated, the constitutional protection of free speech 'means that the government has no power to restrict expression because of its message, its ideas, its subject matter or its content'.[6]

See also: **Genocide, Ku Klux Klan, Xenophobia, ZOG**

Imperialism

The conquest and resurgence of indigenous peoples

Imperialism is the eternal and immutable law of life. All things considered, it is only the need, the wish, and the will to expand that which each individual, each lively and vital people carries in itself.

Benito Mussolini, Fascist Italian leader 1925-43.[1]

● ● ●

Imperialism has been an important theme in the history of almost all nations. Many have been conquered; many have been conquerors; some have, at different times, been both.

The primary purposes of imperialism were to benefit the economic and military interests of the conqueror. These can be characterised as racist because the conquering nations asserted or merely assumed that their interests overrode any rights of the subjugated and racially distinct peoples. Thus, for example, the justification for German colonisation of South West Africa in the early 20th century by colonial official, Dr Paul Rohrbach:

By no argument whatsoever can it be shown that the preservation of any degree of national independence, national prosperity and political organisation by the races of South West Africa, would be of a greater or even of an equal advantage for the development of mankind in general or of the German people in particular, than the making of [such] races serviceable in the enjoyment of their former possessions by the white races.[2]

47

European lawyers developed a doctrine called *terra nullius* ('land belonging to no-one') which deemed it lawful for nations to take control of territory whose inhabitants were considered so 'uncivilised' as to lack a recognisable legal claim to the land on which they lived. According to the Privy Council – the British Empire's highest court – in 1919, the indigenous people of Southern Rhodesia [now Zimbabwe] were 'so low in the scale of social organization [that] it would be idle to impute to such people some shadow of the rights known to our law and then to transmute it into the substance of transferable rights of property as we know them'.[3]

Imperialism was also inspired – or at least justified – by benevolent motives that also involved the denigration of indigenous peoples. Missionaries sought to convert indigenous peoples to Christianity in order to save them and educators dedicated themselves to bring the benefits of civilisation to those whom they considered backward. 'The extinction of the Indians as *Indians* is the ultimate end of Canadian Indian policy', an official of the Bureau of Indian Affairs explained in the mid-20th century.[4]

Imperialists generally used force and the threat of force to conquer and to maintain control. Indigenous peoples who were not valued or who refused to submit faced expulsion or extermination – in the language of today, **ethnic cleansing** and **genocide**. That was the message of Tecumseh ('Cougar Crouching for His Prey'), leader of the Shawnees, who travelled through North America seeking to rally the indigenous peoples to fight the spread of the white settlers in the early 19th century:

The way, the only way, to check and stop this evil is for all Redmen to unite in claiming a common and equal right in the land, as was at first and should yet be... Where today are the Pequot? Where are the Narragansett, the Mohican, the Pokanoket, and many other once powerful tribes of our people? They have vanished before the avarice and the oppression of the White Man, as snow before a summer sun.[5]

Imperial powers and private companies also acquired territory through treaties with indigenous peoples. However, the indigenous peoples commonly entered into such agreements under duress, ceding territorial control in return for promises of protection against the growing numbers of hunters, farmers and miners who entered their lands without agreement.

Treaties drafted by Europeans contained legal concepts with

An Innu woman from Eastern Canada protesting outside the Canadian Air Force Base at Goose Island Bay, Labrador.

© Bob Bartel/Survival International

which the indigenous peoples were not familiar. In New Zealand, for example, Maori chiefs ceded sovereignty over their territories to the British in the Treaty of Waitangi in 1840. The English version of the treaty (the Maori language version differed) guaranteed the Maori what they most valued, 'the full exclusive and undisturbed possession of their Lands', and asked them to give away something apparently worthless, sovereignty.

The cultures of indigenous peoples were destroyed incidentally – for example, by depriving them of sacred territory and hunting grounds – and intentionally, by measures such as the prohibition of native **languages** and the removal of children from their families.

In a number of colonies, particularly those inhabited by hunter-gatherers, the impact of murder, expulsion and newly introduced diseases suggested to observers that the indigenous peoples were completely doomed. 'Our plain duty as good compassionate colonists is to smooth down their dying pillow,' noted Dr Isaac Featherston, the Superintendent of Wellington, New Zealand, in 1856.[6]

The end of empires – illusion and reality

In Australia, New Zealand, South Africa and throughout the Americas, colonialism ended when power was taken by people who immigrated after those countries were conquered by European states, and their descendants. However, the transformation of colonies into independent states did not change the situation of the indigenous peoples. The new rulers continued and sometimes intensified measures to control the land, the resources and the indigenous peoples them-selves. Reviewing the situation in the Americas in the mid-1990s, Phillip Wearne observed that 'disease, military conquest, multinational capitalism, religious conversion... the indigenous peoples of the Americas are today losing life and land to the same forces that have devastated their numbers and culture for more than five hundred years'.[7] It is estimated that during the course of the 20th century, 90 of more than 200 indigenous tribes who lived in the Amazon basin disappeared.[8]

Over 300 Guarani – Brazilian Indians – committed suicide in the 15 years immediately prior to 2000. The youngest was Luciane Ortiz, aged nine. Rosalino Ortiz says:

The Guarani are committing suicide because we have no land. We don't have space any more. In the old days we were free, now we are no longer free. So our young people look around them and think there is nothing left and wonder how they can live. They sit down and think, they lose themselves and then commit suicide.[9]

A notice advertising Indian land for sale, 1910.

'Return of the Indian'

On 12 October 1992, 500 years after Columbus landed in the Americas, thousands of indigenous people rallied to demonstrate their strengthening opposition to the effects of the conquest. Javier Albo describes what has occurred in the Americas as 'the return of the Indian'.[10]

In other regions as well, indigenous peoples have become vocal and visible domestically and internationally in their campaigns for civil, political, economic, social and cultural rights. Some seek rights taken from their forbears centuries ago; some seek rights lost within their own lifetime. They have used all manner of techniques to pursue their claims, including legal action to enforce treaties whose terms had been violated for so long that they had come to be regarded as only of historical interest.

Their campaigns have often provoked violent responses from governments, landowners, miners and others with interests to protect. Many indigenous people and their supporters, have been killed, tortured and imprisoned.

See also: **Ethnic cleansing, Genocide, Language, On the Origin of Species, Volk, White Man's Burden**

J'accuse

It is a crime to misdirect public opinion and to pervert it until it becomes delirious. It is a crime to poison small and simple minds, to rouse the passions of intolerance and reaction through the medium of the miserable anti-semitism of which great and liberal France, with her Rights of Man, will expire if she is not soon cured. It is a crime to exploit patriotism for motives of hatred and it is a crime, finally, to make of the sword the modern god when all human science is at work to bring about a future of truth and justice.

Émile Zola, 1898

On 13 January 1898, *J'accuse* ('I accuse') appeared in large bold type across the front page of the Parisian newspaper *L'Aurore*. Below the headline was a lengthy open letter from the renowned French writer Émile Zola to Félix Faure, President of France. Zola's letter denounced the perversion of justice in the conviction of French soldier Captain Alfred Dreyfus as a spy.

In 1894, the French counter-intelligence service discovered that secrets had been passed to the German embassy in Paris. Suspicion fell on Dreyfus, a Jew. Dreyfus protested his innocence but a secret court-martial convicted him of treason. He was sentenced to life imprisonment and sent to Devil's Island.

Anti-semitism was widespread in France. When the newspaper *La Libre Parole* suggested that Dreyfus's alleged espionage demonstrated

Jewish treachery, it both reflected and confirmed popular opinion.

Two years after Dreyfus was convicted, strong evidence emerged that another officer, Major Ferdinand Walsin Esterhazy, was the spy. Army chief of intelligence Lieutenant Colonel Georges Picquart tried to reopen the case despite opposition from his superiors. For his efforts, Picquart was transferred to Tunisia. Esterhazy was court-martialled in January 1898 but was unanimously acquitted by the seven judges after five minutes deliberation. Outside the court, a crowd joyfully greeted the news. Their chants included 'death to the Jews!'.

Émile Zola was shocked and angered by the conspiracy of officials to suppress the truth. Dreyfus was the immediate victim but the case concerned more than the fate of an individual - the fundamental rights of the nation were at stake. *J'accuse* split the nation. It inspired many to campaign for Dreyfus; others became more convinced that the case was evidence of a Jewish conspiracy.

In February 1898, Zola was prosecuted for libelling the army and was sentenced to imprisonment. Premier Meline told the Parliament: *The Jews who foolishly unloosed this prepared campaign of hatred, brought down upon themselves a century of intolerance – the Jews and that intellectual elite which seems to enjoy poisoning the atmosphere and inciting bloody hatred.*[1]

Zola fled to England where he remained until he received an amnesty. Information emerged that an army officer had forged evidence used against Dreyfus, but a new court-martial convicted Dreyfus again in 1899. 'That Dreyfus was a traitor I conclude from his race,' observed the prominent French nationalist Maurice Barrés.[2] In the following years further information undermined the prosecution case and in 1906 a court completely cleared Dreyfus.

On 20 July 1906, Dreyfus was awarded the Chevalier of the Legion d'Honneur in the same courtyard where, as convicted traitor, he had been stripped of his sword. To the crowd who shouted 'Vive Dreyfus' [Long live Dreyfus] he replied, 'Non, messiuex, je vous en prie:Vive la France'. [No - long live France] In 1943 his granddaughter Madeleine was sent to the Auschwitz concentration camp where she died.

The so-called Dreyfus Affair occurred a century ago in France, but its lessons are of universal and continuing importance. The first is that racial prejudice profoundly corrupts and damages society. The justice system failed because the guilt or innocence of Dreyfus could not be fairly determined when community leaders, sections of the

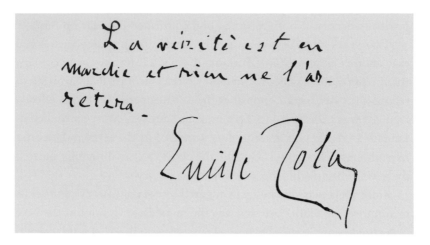

'Truth is on the march and nothing can stop it'. Note written by Zola.

media and much of public opinion openly condemned all members of his race as untrustworthy. As philosopher Charles Péguy has noted, a failure of this kind casts a shadow upon a society at large:

...a single injustice, a single illegality, especially if it be officially confirmed, especially if it be generally, nationally, conveniently accepted, is enough to dishonour and disgrace an entire nation.[3]

The second lesson is the courage and tenacity required by Zola and others who campaigned to expose the scandal and to secure redress for Dreyfus. They were prosecuted, they were abused and they were threatened. But in the end, they prevailed.

In 1984, the Human Rights Institute of the Bar of Bordeaux and the European Lawyers Union established the Ludovic Trarieux International Human Rights Prize. This is awarded to lawyers who have defended human rights and worked against racism and intolerance. Ludovic Trarieux was a lawyer who defended Dreyfus and opposed anti-semitism. Immediately following Zola's trial, Trarieux established an organisation, the *Ligue des Droits de L'homme et du Citoyen* – League for the Rights of Man and the Citizen.

The first person to receive the prize was South African anti-apartheid leader Nelson Mandela. In 2000 the prize was awarded to Turkish writer and lawyer Esber Yagmurdereli, who was imprisoned in 1998 because he made a speech criticising the government's treatment of the Kurdish minority. Following an international campaign, Esber Yagmurdereli was released on 18 January 2001.

Deuxième Année. — Numéro 87

Cinq Centimes

JEUDI 13 JANVIER 1898

Directeur
ERNEST VAUGHAN
ABONNEMENTS

POUR LA RÉDACTION
S'adresser à M. A. BERTHIER
Secrétaire de la Rédaction

Directeur
ERNEST VAUGHAN
LES ANNONCES SONT REÇUES :
143 — Rue Montmartre — 143

ADRESSER LETTRES ET MANDATS
À M. A. BOUT, Administrateur
Téléphone : 109-86

L'AURORE

Littéraire, Artistique, Sociale

J'Accuse...!

LETTRE AU PRÉSIDENT DE LA RÉPUBLIQUE

Par ÉMILE ZOLA

LETTRE
A M. FÉLIX FAURE
Président de la République

Monsieur le Président,

Me permettez-vous, dans ma gratitude pour le bienveillant accueil que vous m'avez fait un jour, d'avoir le souci de votre juste gloire et de vous dire que votre étoile, si heureuse jusqu'ici, est menacée de la plus honteuse, de la plus ineffaçable des taches?

[The remainder of the page consists of the multi-column text of Émile Zola's open letter, printed in small type across six columns.]

Front page of Paris newspaper *L'Aurore* in which Zola denounced the conviction of Captain Dreyfus in 1898.

Ku Klux Klan

Racist organisations

It's evident to any one with common sense that America was founded as a white Christian nation. This doesn't mean we want to scare or hurt non-whites. It means simply that America would be governed according to the tenets of Christianity. This would benefit all who lived within her boundaries whether a white citizen or a non-white resident.

Thomas Robb of the Knights of the Ku Klux Klan.[1]

'Ku Klux Klan' is the oldest name continuously associated with overtly racist organisations. The first Ku Klux Klan group was set up in the USA following the Civil War of 1861-65, which brought an end to slavery in that country. Many white people in the defeated southern states were determined to maintain the subordination of black people. To pursue this aim, around 1865 a small group of former Confederate (southern) army officers in Tennessee set up an organisation they called Ku Klux Klan, adapted from the Greek word *kuklos* – 'circle'.

In the following decades the organisation spread and was notoriously violent. Klan groups terrorised black people to deter them from exercising their civil rights and targeted white people whom they considered to be traitors to their race. The original Klan

● Imperial Knights of Australian Ku Klux Klan, meeting in Sydney 2001.

faded in the early 20th century and its name, rituals and ideology were adopted by a new organisation, the Knights of the Ku Klux Klan. As well as blacks, the Knights targeted Catholics, Jews and people considered to be politically 'liberal' or left wing, such as trade unionists.

At its peak in the 1920s, the Knights of the Ku Klux Klan had an estimated three to four million members. Its membership declined and other organisations have been set up using the Klan title. At the beginning of the 21st century there were more than 100 groups in the USA with Ku Klux Klan or Klan in their names but their total membership was estimated to be fewer than 5,000 people.

A number of the Klan groups are attempting to establish a respectable reputation, disclaiming violence, openly supporting candidates for political office and even participating in a highway beautification program so that their contribution will be publicly acknowledged on roadway signs. Several states rejected Klan groups' applications to join the programme but in 2001 the US Supreme Court ruled that Klan groups are entitled to participate because of the constitutional protection of freedom of speech.

There are hundreds of other overtly racist groups in the USA, including so-called 'skinhead gangs' [because they shave their heads], neo-Nazi groups and publishers of racist literature and music.[2]

Racist groups are numerous and diverse in Europe as well. As in the US, there are violent skinhead and neo-Nazi gangs, and so-called 'white power' bands whose concerts and CDs raise money for racist organisations.

In a number of European countries, political parties whose electoral platforms are intended to exploit racism and xenophobia have won seats on local, national and regional legislatures and their influence on issues such as immigration has been significant. In France, for example, the Front National (FN) formed by Jean-Marie Le Pen in 1972, has campaigned for policies such as the repatriation of immigrants and won 14 per cent of the national vote in 1986.

In 2001, the European Union imposed diplomatic sanctions on Austria because of the participation in its government of the Freedom Party, which was accused of inciting racism and xenophobia. The action was condemned as hypocritical by the Freedom Party's leader Jörg Haider, who contended that his party's policies were similar to those of countries whose governments were critical of him.

Combating racist organisations

Generally governments combat racist organisations in two ways – by prohibiting hate speech, and by banning organisations – for example, several European countries have banned overtly Nazi organisations and Israel banned Kach, a violently anti-Arab organisation.

The major international anti-racist treaty, the 1966 Convention on the Elimination of Racial Discrimination, states that governments should use both measures.

While many have imposed some restrictions on hate speech there has been far less inclination to ban organisations. This reluctance reflects two considerations. First, as a matter of principle, that banning organisations would violate the right of freedom of association. Secondly, that such action might be *ineffective* – it is better, some argue, to permit racist groups to operate openly so that their activities can be monitored and opposed.

Governmental agencies have the lead role in response to racists who commit crimes. Non-governmental organisations and individuals are generally the most active opponents of racists in all other areas – their main techniques include:

- Disseminating information to counter the views propagated by racists, such as on the alleged criminality of immigrants and racial minorities;
- Monitoring racists' activities – this has enabled non-governmental organisations to, for example, expose racist groups seeking to infiltrate 'respectable' non-racist organisations;
- Physical confrontation – racist groups march and rally in public places to intimidate racial minorities and to appear powerful. Anti-racist groups respond by blocking the routes of racist marches and breaking up racist meetings.

The less common technique of civil litigation has been used by a US organisation, the Southern Poverty Law Center. In Alabama in 1981, Michael Donald, a young black man, was abducted, beaten and lynched by two members of the United Klans of America. The two Klansmen were convicted for the murder. The Law Center acted on behalf of Beulah Mae Donald, Michael's mother, to sue the United Klans, which had a long history of racist violence. The United Klans and the men who murdered Michael Donald were ordered to pay Beulah Mae Donald US$7 million in damages and as a result the United Klans group was forced to turn its headquarters over to her. The Southern Poverty Law Center has won other cases against racist organisations that have resulted in awards of large sums in damages.[3]

Combating racist governments

Governments have been very loathe to pressure other governments to cease racist conduct and have generally done so only following sustained lobbying from their own citizens. The 1948 Genocide Convention provides a basis under international law for countries to intervene to stop genocide occurring but its provisions have never been invoked. Among the few significant international actions during the last 50 years against racism by governments towards their own citizens are:

- the imposition of sanctions on the white minority regime that seized power in Rhodesia (now Zimbabwe), 1966 to 1979;
- the imposition of sanctions on South Africa for its apartheid policies, 1977 to 1994;
- military intervention by NATO in response to Serb persecution of ethnic Albanians in the Yugoslavian province of Kosovo, in 1999.[4]
- UN forces intervened in East Timor in 1999, to protect pro-independence East Timorese people from attack by anti-independence Indonesian forces and Indonesia-backed paramilitaries.

Non-governmental groups and individuals have also used a wide range of techniques to oppose racist authorities in their own countries and internationally. They too have had to confront the issue of whether or not to use violence.

See also: **Hate speech, Non-violence, Xenophobia, Yellow Peril, ZOG**

Language

My father, who attended Alberni Indian Residential School for four years in the twenties, was physically tortured by his teachers for speaking Tseshaht: they pushed sewing needles through his tongue, a routine punishment for language offenders... The needle tortures suffered by my father affected all my family. My Dad's attitude became 'why teach my children Indian if they are going to be punished for speaking it?' so he would not allow my mother to speak Indian to us in his presence. I never learned how to speak my own language. I am now, therefore, truly a 'dumb Indian'.

Randy Fred, First Nation (indigenous) Canadian, 1980s.[1]

In the first half of the 16th century, the English were determined to crush recurrent Welsh rebellion against their rule. One of the sources of unrest, the English believed, was the persistence of Welsh identity based on the Welsh language. According to the 1536 Act of Union which annexed Wales to England, 'because the people do daily use a speech nothing like nor consonant to the Mother tongue used within this Realm, some rude and ignorant people have made distinction between the King's subjects of this realm and his subjects of Wales'.[2] The Welsh language was therefore to be destroyed, and ceased to be a language of offical use.

Three hundred years later, further harsh measures were imposed, for

● No to Afrikaans: School students protest in Soweto, South Africa in June 1976. Opposition to the apartheid government's black education policies exploded when it was ordered that lessons like maths and history must be taught in Afrikaans, the oppressor's language.

© The World Newspapers/Soweto, 1976

rather different reasons. In 1847, the report of an inquiry into Welsh education concluded that the Welsh language was inferior, vulgar and backward. The use of Welsh in schools was prohibited and a child caught speaking the language was required to wear a piece of wood hung around their neck with a leather strap. The piece of wood, which became known as the 'Welsh Not', was passed to any other child who spoke Welsh and the child who had it at the end of the day was beaten.[3]

In reaction to English attempts to destroy Welsh, the protection of the language became a key issue for Welsh nationalists. In a campaign starting in the 1960s, campaigners destroyed and painted over English street and place names until the authorities allowed them to be bilingual, they refused to pay tax and bills until the official forms were bilingual, and they sabotaged television stations until a Welsh-speaking channel was established.[4]

As the following cases illustrate, English suppression of the Welsh language is mirrored in the actions of dominant groups in many other countries over the centuries. There have been both similar motives – the destruction of a group's identity for political reasons or because its culture is considered inferior – and similar methods, such as prohibiting children from using their mother tongue in school.

France Though cultural assimilation had been a long-standing aim of French government, at the time of the French Revolution in 1789 a government report estimated that almost half of the population either did not know French or could not converse in it. Government members feared that linguistic diversity was a threat to the revolution and to national unity. A number of measures were proposed to promote French and weaken other languages including the suppression of non-French publications and commercial signs, the dismissal of provincial public officials who did not speak French and forcible transfers of population.[5]

In the French colonies as well, language was seen as a means of control. 'Above all else,' a colonial governor noted in 1921, 'education proposes to expand the influence of the French language, in order to establish the [French] nationality or culture in Africa.'[6]

Spain During the civil war in the 1930s, Euskera, the Basque language, gained official recognition when the province had a brief period of autonomy. But the republican forces that the Basques strongly supported were defeated and the victors, led by General Franco, imposed a crackdown. 'My brothers and I were beaten at school if we were caught speaking Euskera, the language we spoke at home,' recalls Basque writer Bernard Atxaga. 'We knew we risked punishment if we spoke Basque in public.'[7] The Basque territory regained autonomy and restored the official status of the language after the dictatorship established by Franco fell in 1975.

Bulgaria In the early 1970s, the Bulgarian government sought to promote the assimilation of the large ethnic Turkish population by merging Turkish language schools with Bulgarian schools and stopping Turkish being taught in Bulgarian schools. In the 1980s, the government embarked on a more aggressive assimilation campaign with measures that included fining people for speaking Turkish in public and forcing ethnic Turks to change their names to ethnic Bulgarian names. Many ethnic Turks who opposed the assimilation campaign reportedly lost their jobs or were imprisoned, forcibly resettled or killed.[8]

Turkey In its efforts to suppress demands for independence by its Kurdish minority, Turkey prohibited Kurdish language publications until 1991 and still prohibits broadcasting in Kurdish. According to Turkish Deputy Prime Minister Devlet Bahceli: 'It is not possible for Turkey to look warmly at cultural and ethnic rights that can fuel ethnic clashes and division.'[9]

Colonial and post-colonial schools At various times continuing well into the 20th century, schools in a number of colonial and former colonial countries banned indigenous children from speaking their native languages because the languages were considered inferior and their use a barrier to assimilation. 'So long as he keeps his native tongue, so long will he remain a community apart,' the Canadian Department of Indian Affairs reported in 1895.[10] Describing his schooldays in the 1960s, Kenyan novelist Mwangi wa Mutahi recalls children being beaten and temporarily expelled for speaking or writing in Gikuyu and other African languages: '[i]n the mind of my educators, African languages were not actually languages but primitive vernaculars.'[11]

Anthropologist Hugh Brody has remarked on the fact that within the British Empire there was a different attitude towards indigenous languages in colonies inhabited by agriculturalists – much of India, Africa and Southeast Asia – and in colonies inhabited by hunter-gathers, such as those in North America, Australia and southern Africa. In the former, English tended to be taught as an addition to existing languages whereas in the latter it was imposed as the sole language.[12]

Brody believes that the difference reflects a fundamental difference in how Europeans perceived the two groups. In the agriculturalist colonies, 'European conquerors were dealing with farmers like themselves' and their main aim was to extract profit from the existing populations. Hunter-gathers and their societies were quite alien to Europeans and were rival claimants to the land the colonialists wanted to settle. As such they 'had to be silenced or removed', and the destruction of the indigenous languages was a means of eliminating the opposition. 'To secure an uninhabited land, there must be no minds in the way, no rival words that imply enduring presence and deep claims to the place.'[13]

See also: **Imperialism, Volk**

Miscegenation

Who, that has any decency, can help being shocked at the familiar intercourse, which has gradually been gaining ground, and which has, at last, got a complete footing between the Negroes and the women of England? No black swain need, in this loving country, hang himself in despair. No inquiry is made whether he be a pagan or a Christian; if he be not a downright cripple he will, if he be so disposed, always find a woman, not merely to yield to his filthy embraces, that, amongst the notoriously polluted and abandoned part of the sex, would be less shocking, but to accompany him to the altar, to become his wife, to breed English mulattoes, to stamp the mark of Cain upon her family and her country!

William Cobbett, renowned campaigner for rights of rural labourers and working-class people in England, 1804. [1]

• • •

In June 1958, Mildred Jeter and Richard Loving married in Washington, District of Columbia. They were residents of Virginia, adjacent to Washington DC, but could not marry there because Mildred Jeter was black and Richard Loving was white. A law of the state – originally the Racial Integrity Act of 1924 – prohibited marriage between white and non-white people. The law also prohibited people from leaving the state to evade the prohibition.

The Lovings were prosecuted and sentenced to one year in jail, suspended for 25 years if they left Virginia and did not return for 25

● Cuxhaven, Germany 1933: Nazis force Jewish man Oskar Danker and his friend Christian woman Adele E to wear signs to discourage non-Jews and Jews from mixing. Her sign reads 'I am fit for the greatest swine and only get involved with Jews' and his 'As a Jew, I only take German girls to my room'.

© Getty Images Inc

years. In his decision the trial judge stated:

Almighty God created the races white, black, yellow, malay and red, and he placed them on separate continents. And but for the interference with his arrangement there would be no cause for such marriages. The fact that he separated the races shows that he did not intend for the races to mix.[2]

The Lovings were clearly not convinced that the Virginia legislature was divinely inspired when it prohibited interracial marriage. They left the state and initiated legal action, asserting that the law violated the US Constitution, which bars racial discrimination by the state and the federal government. In 1967 the US Supreme Court ruled that the law was indeed unconstitutional.[3] The fact that the law prohibited only interracial marriages involving white people, the court noted, demonstrated that the law was 'designed to maintain White Supremacy'.

The Supreme Court's decision invalidated Virginia's law and similar laws in 15 other states, ending a form of racism that had been initiated three centuries previously in Maryland. Fourteen states had repealed laws outlawing interracial marriages in the 15 years prior to the court's decision. One by one the remaining states repealed their now unenforceable laws. The last to do so was Alabama, by referendum in November 2000. Forty per cent – 544,000 people – voted to retain it.

The Supreme Court described these laws as 'miscegenation' statutes, using a term that had been coined in the USA just over a century earlier, when the country was in the midst of a fierce civil war involving another aspect of relations between its white and black people, that of slavery. In 1863 an anonymous leaflet was published, advocating the benefits of black and white couples having children together.[4] To describe the theory, the anonymous author created the word 'miscegenation' from the Latin words miscere – to 'mix' – and genus – 'race'.

The pamphlet urged President Lincoln to campaign for miscegenation in the presidential election to be held in 1864. Lincoln represented the Republican Party and his Democrat opponents sought to exploit white racism by claiming that the pamphlet reflected Republican views. Republicans suspected that the pamphlet was spurious and designed to harm them politically. Their suspicions were confirmed following the election – which the Republicans won – when it was revealed that the authors were Democrats. The hoax failed but left a permanent legacy to the English language.

State governments of the USA were neither the first nor the last in the world to prohibit interracial marriages and the prohibitions were not restricted to white and black marriages. In South Africa, interracial marriage was prohibited in 1685. Extra-marital sexual relations between 'Europeans' and 'Coloureds' were prohibited in 1923. The prohibitions were extended to marriages between whites and coloureds or Indians in 1949 and a year later all sexual contact between whites and non-whites was made illegal. Eleven thousand people were convicted between 1950 and 1985. Helen Suzman, a persistent opponent of the laws in the South African Parliament, attributed many suicides as well as broken families and social ostracism to the humiliation people incurred as a result of the publicity of being prosecuted.[5]

Nazi Germany introduced the Law for the Protection of German Blood and German Honour in 1935, prohibiting marriage between

'Aryans' and 'non-Aryans' the latter being mainly Jews and Roma. Germany's Second World War ally Croatia followed suit, an ironic policy as the Nazis considered Croatians to be non-Aryan. The Croatian law also prohibited sexual relations between male Jews and female Croats. Croatian men were not prohibited from sexual relations with Jewish women, a telling gender distinction.

Laws banning interracial marriage and sexual relations have disappeared but unlegislated sanctions can be severe. In 1990, extremist Hutus in Rwanda published 'The Ten Commandments of the Hutu', which included the following injunction:

Every Hutu should know that a Tutsi woman, wherever she is, works for the interest of her Tutsi ethnic group. As a result, we shall consider a traitor any Hutu who: marries a Tutsi woman; befriends a Tutsi woman; employs a Tutsi woman as a secretary or concubine.[6]

During the genocide conducted against the Tutsis in 1994, many Hutu 'traitors' were also killed.

In Germany in 2001, three skinheads were convicted of attempting to murder a former colleague because – according to one of the perpetrators – the victim had 'betrayed the right-wing ideology because he had sex with a foreign woman'.[7] According to a media report, she was described as 'dark-skinned' in court testimony but her nationality was not revealed.[8]

The impact of the disquiet that interracial mixing continues to evoke is evident in less dramatic ways as well. In Britain in 2000, a woman wrote to a personal advice columnist in a national newspaper because her father opposed her forthcoming marriage to a black man. Her father said he was against the marriage because 'it would be unfair to bring up a child of mixed race'. The writer wanted to know, 'does my father have a point?' The columnist urged her to marry the man she loves; readers' responses were divided.[9] Across the Atlantic, producers of pornography were drawing up new guidelines banning certain plots in the hope of dissuading US authorities from an anti-pornography drive. One of the guidelines provides: 'No black men, white women themes.'[10]

See also: **Apartheid, Caste**

Non-violence

Dear Friend – Before embarking on civil disobedience and taking the risk I have dreaded to take all these years I would fain approach you and find a way out. My personal faith is absolutely clear. I cannot intentionally hurt anything that lives, much less fellow human beings, even though they may do the greatest wrong to me and mine. Whilst, therefore, I hold British rule to be a curse, I do not intend to harm a single Englishman or any legitimate interest he may have in India... I know that in embarking on non-violence, I shall be running what might fairly be termed a mad risk, but the victories of truth have never been won without risks, often of the gravest character... If people join me, as I expect they will, the sufferings they will undergo unless the British nation sooner retraces its steps, will be enough to melt the stoniest hearts...

Letter from Indian independence leader, Mohandas Gandhi, to the Viceroy of India in 1930, informing him of an impending campaign against government control of the production of salt, which increased its price.[1]

● ● ●

Gandhi developed a philosophy of non-violent opposition to authority when he led a movement against the racial discrimination experienced by Indians in South Africa, where he lived in the late 19th and early 20th centuries. Gandhi considered non-violence to be an important moral principle, not simply a tactic dictated by weakness. As such, he asserted,

● Indian nationalist leader Mahatma Gandhi (centre) leading march in protest against the government monopoly of salt production.

it was quite different to what was commonly described as 'passive resistance' and he coined the term 'Satyagraha' – derived from Sanskrit – to emphasise the distinction:

Truth (Satya) implies love, and firmness (agraha) engenders and therefore serves as a synonym for force. I thus began to call the Indian movement 'Satyagraha'. That is to say the Force which is born of Truth and love or non-violence...[2]

He returned to India in 1915 and his advocacy of Satyagraha made non-violence an important strand of the independence movement. It was however, not the only one. Other activists were not persuaded that Satyagraha was either morally superior or particularly effective and at various times the independence campaign was marked by severe violence before the British left India in 1947.

Gandhi's campaigning made him an internationally renowned figure. In 1935 he received a group of black visitors and remarked that 'perhaps it will be through the Negro that the unadulterated message of non-violence will be delivered to the whole world'.[3] His observation was prophetic. In the 1950s and 1960s, Reverend Martin

Luther King adopted Gandhian ideas in shaping the strategy of the Civil Rights Movement's campaign against anti-black discrimination: *Boycotting buses in Montgomery, demonstrating in Birmingham, the citadel of segregation; and defying guns, dogs, and clubs in Selma, while maintaining disciplined non-violence, totally confused the rulers of the South. If they let us march, they admitted their lie that the black man was content. If they shot us down, they told the world they were inhuman brutes.*[4]

Other black leaders argued that violence was essential to defend blacks against racist violence. In 1964 the Organization of Afro-American Unity was established to campaign for black rights and its charter included a declaration of 'Self Defense', asserting 'in those areas where the government is either unable or unwilling to protect the lives and property of our people... our people are within their rights to protect themselves by whatever means necessary.' At the organisation's founding rally, Malcolm X, one of its leaders, stated:
The time for you and me to allow ourselves to be brutalised non-violently is passé. *Be nonviolent only with those who are nonviolent to you. And when you can bring me a nonviolent racist, bring me a nonviolent segregationist, then I'll get nonviolent... If the United States government doesn't want you and me to get rifles, then take those rifles away from those racists. If they don't want you and me to use clubs, take the clubs away from those racists. If they don't want you and me to get violent, then stop the racists from being violent. Don't teach us nonviolence while those crackers are violent. Those days are over.*[5]

Over several years from 1965, blacks rioted in many American cities, fuelled by a volatile mix of anger and frustration at poverty, discrimination and police brutality as well as radical ideas commonly identified with the term 'Black Power'. In April 1968 King was assassinated. His murder sparked rioting across the nation.

Gandhi's ideas were also influential in the evolution of the campaign against apartheid in South Africa, where Satyagraha was born. However, after decades of political struggle and civil disobedience, in the 1960s anti-apartheid leaders concluded that non-violence would not succeed. On trial charged with sabotage and plotting to overthrow the government, Nelson Mandela told the Supreme Court of South Africa that black African leaders had come to the view that 'it would be

Nelson Mandela and Walter Sisulu, Robben Island prison, 1966. They were serving life sentences for sabotage.

© Mayibuye Centre

unrealistic and wrong for African leaders to continue preaching peace and non-violence at a time when the Government met our peaceful demands with force'. They therefore formed an organisation to embark on armed struggle and issued a statement – the Manifesto of Umkhonto – explaining their decision:

The time comes in the life of any nation when there remain only two choices – submit or fight. That time has now come to South Africa. We shall not submit and we have no choice but to hit back by all means in our power in defence of our people, our future and our freedom.[6]

Whether or not to use violence continues to be a critical moral and strategic issue facing campaigners against racism and other human rights violations.

See also: **Apartheid, Ku Klux Klan**

On the Origin of Species

When two races of men meet, they act precisely like two species of animals – they fight each other, bring diseases to each other &c, but then comes the more deadly struggle, namely which have the best fitted organization, or instincts (ie intellect in man) to gain the day.

Charles Darwin[1]

●   ●   ●

In 1859, Charles Darwin published *On the Origin of Species by Means of Natural Selection, or the Preservation of Favoured Races in the Struggle for Life*. The book presented in detail the theory of evolution, which proposed that species develop because there is a struggle for existence that is won by individuals with 'advantageous' characteristics. The winners are more likely to procreate than the losers and so their advantageous characteristics will predominate in future generations. The 'injurious' traits of the losers will therefore tend to disappear. 'This preservation of favourable individual differences and variations, and the destruction of those which are injurious,' Darwin stated, 'I have called Natural Selection, or the Survival of the Fittest.'[2]

The races referred to in the title of Darwin's book were not the human race or human races, but the theory was clearly as applicable to people as to other creatures. Just over a decade later, Darwin examined human evolution in *The Descent of Man*. The theory of evolution as expounded by Darwin and people who adopted it has influenced perceptions of the nature of race, of racial differences and

● During the conquest of the Americas, the Spanish used dogs against the indigenous peoples – illustration by Theodor de Bry, 1592. Charles Darwin suggested that '[a]t some future period not very distant as measured in centuries, the civilised races of man will almost certainly exterminate and replace throughout the world the savage races'.3

of relations between races. Darwinian ideas have been significant in a number of areas, three of which are described below.

The origin of races

In the 19th century there were two schools of thought about the origins of different races of people. 'Polygenists' contended that races were quite distinct species. 'Monogenists' believed that races had developed from common origins. Darwin was a monogenist. Current research into the genetic makeup of different human populations confirms Darwin's view that all people are fundamentally similar. According to biologist Svante Pääbo:

*The general picture already apparent from [large-scale comparisons of human genomes] is that the gene pool in Africa contains more variation then elsewhere, and that the genetic variation found outside of Africa represents only a subset of that found within the African continent. From a genetic perspective, all humans are therefore Africans, either residing in Africa or in recent exile.*4

Conflict between races

While Darwin considered that the similarities between races demonstrated a common origin, the differences were significant for the relations between races. Just like other species, people competed with each other and in the struggle for life 'the grade of their civilization seems to be a most important element in the success of competing nations'.[5] He described the grades as 'civilised' and 'classical' on the one hand and 'barbarians' and 'savages' on the other. As was the case with other species, Darwin believed, the consequences of defeat included extinction.

Darwin's ideas were widely applied to the analysis of domestic and international events.[6] Known as 'social Darwinism', it could also be used to advocate political policies such as imperialism. Here is how a pamphlet of the 1905 Marseille Colonial Exhibition described what was occurring in the French Empire:

When we have done our task of kind civilized people towards the weak, we will then just have to bend to the irreversible natural law which suppresses the population ill-adapted to the struggle for life, and then exploit the lands freed by the extinction of our subjects of black race... If the natives keep on leading their careless life they will leave their place to the more energetic races from Europe.[7]

The notion of races and nations locked in a life and death struggle has persisted in various forms into the present century. For Sister Lisa, Women's Director of the 'World Church of the Creator':

Our White Brothers and Sisters in America (and worldwide) have been lulled into a false sense of security about their racial futures. They do not understand just how close we really are to that huge iceberg, nor do they understand that when the ship (our nation) strikes the iceberg, (racial disaster), the ship will go down just as fast, with just as many deadly consequences, as happened on the Titanic herself... Those of us who are racially aware... are able to see that iceberg ahead, we can prepare, and we have a sacred mandate to warn them of the impending disaster. If they will not heed our words, then we know that their fate is sealed in the dark waters of the mud races which will wash over them and drag them down to the depths.[8]

Eugenics

British scientist Sir Francis Galton, a cousin of Darwin, soon recognised the implications of the theory of evolution for society: the health of populations could be improved through selective parent-hood. In 1883 he coined the term 'eugenics', from the Greek for 'good birth' or 'origins', to describe his ideas and defined it as 'the study of the agencies under social control, that improve or impair the racial qualities of future generations either physically or mentally'.[9]

Eugenic ideas found receptive and influential audiences in many countries. In 1907, the state of Indiana in the USA was the first government to implement eugenics coercively when it legislated to permit the sterilisation of mentally handicapped people. Twenty-six other USA states had similar laws by 1931. European governments were also impressed by the US approach. The Swiss Canton of Vaud in 1928; Denmark in 1929; Finland in 1930; Germany in 1933; Sweden in 1935 and other jurisdictions passed laws permitting the sterilisation of people with mental handicaps.

Advocates of eugenics commonly stated that it would promote racial improvement. In Sweden, for example, eugenics was promoted by the Swedish Institute for Racial Biology established in the 1920s and when the sterilisation programme was introduced people of 'mixed racial quality' and Roma were among those targeted.[10]

Although public support for eugenics was greatly diminished by the brutal manner in which the Nazis had implemented it, compulsory sterilisation programmes continued in Finland until 1955, Denmark until 1967, and Sweden until 1975. Czechoslovakia, according to one commentator, conducted a 'racial eugenics campaign' against the Roma in the 1970s:

(S)tate agents – social workers and medical professionals – took exceptional measures to prevent the Roma from breeding. Material inducements were a popular method. Sometimes Romani woman would be offered cash in return for being sterilised. Sometimes a sort of barter was employed: for example, the state might furnish a Romani flat as its side of the bargain. In other cases... doctors performed sterilisations under cover of other surgical procedures.[11]

Under the 1948 Convention on Genocide, the crime of genocide includes trying to destroy a racial group by imposing measures in order to prevent births.

See also: **Biology, Imperialism, Miscegenation, Porraimos, Yellow Peril, ZOG**

Porraimos

[T]he result of our investigations have allowed us to characterise the Gypsies as being a people of entirely primitive ethnological origins, whose mental backwardness makes them incapable of real social adaptation... The Gypsy question can only be solved when the main body of asocial and worthless Gypsy individuals of mixed blood is collected together in large labour camps and kept working there, and when the further breeding of this population of mixed blood is permanently stopped once and for all. Only then will future generations of the German people be really freed from this burden.

Dr Robert Ritter, head of the Racial Hygiene and Population Biology Research Unit of the German Ministry of Health, 1940.[1]

●   ●   ●

The government heeded Dr Ritter's suggestion that the Roma – commonly called Gypsies, a term many find objectionable – should be forced into camps. Most of their fellow prisoners were Jews and the government planned the same fate for both groups: genocide. Six million Jews were killed and the survivors called their tragedy the Holocaust, the burning of the whole. The number of Roma victims has been estimated as between 500,000 and 1.5 million of a European population of about two million. Survivors of the Roma genocide refer to it as Porraimos, 'the devouring'.

Porraimos was the most extreme event in centuries of persecution of the Roma throughout Europe.[2] In the 17th century, for example,

Dutch police, soldiers and civilians took part in anti-Roma drives called *Heidenjachten* ('heathen-hunts'), a Swedish royal ordinance of 1637 banished all Roma and ordered that those who remained could be executed without trial, while Roma were hanged along the border of the Czech lands to deter any who might want to enter.

In 1721, Emperor Charles VI of the Holy Roman Empire ordered that Roma men were to be executed and women and children were to have an ear cut off. In 1912 France legislated that 'itinerants' must carry identity documents; many communes posted signs at their borders warning *interdit aux nomades* – 'prohibited to nomads'.

Since Porraimos, Roma have continued to be the subject of racist rhetoric and conduct by politicians, public officials, the media and private individuals wherever they live. In the Czech Republic, 69 per cent of respondents to a 1998 poll expressed antipathy towards Roma, 14 per cent wanted all Roma to be deported and only 2 per cent said they would be willing to accept a Romani person into their family.[3]

In several Central and Eastern European countries, Romani children have been disproportionately assigned to schools or to classes for children with mental disabilities. In the Czech Republic, for example, around 70 per cent of Romani children attended special schools in 1999. The routine placement of Romani children in special schools and classes has been described as creating a 'particularly degrading form of segregation... that brands Romani children as mentally defective and consigns them to a life in which their brightest prospect is menial work'.[4]

In recent years, there have been reports of racist gangs attacking Roma – sometimes with fatal consequences – in Albania, Austria, Bosnia, Bulgaria, Croatia, the Czech Republic, Hungary, Italy, Poland, Romania, Russia, the Slovak Republic, Ukraine, and Yugoslavia.[5] Communal violence has occurred in fewer countries but has also had profound effects. In Romania alone, according to one report, 30 Romani communities were destroyed between 1990 and 1995.[6] One attack was reported by Italian media as follows:

[O]n the evening of 18 June 1999, a Romani man visiting the Italian town of Scampia on the northern periphery of Naples seriously injured two local girls riding a motor scooter while driving his car. The driver, who was reportedly drunk, fled the scene of the accident. The next morning, local men described as having shaved heads, earrings and tattoos entered one of the town's six Romani camps and told the inhabitants to 'leave or be burnt with the camp'. They then

● Destruction of Romani dwellings, Casilino 700 Camp, Rome, September 1999

© Stefano Montesi

set the camp on fire. As the camp's one thousand inhabitants fled, neighbours applauded from the nearby balconies. According to camp residents, police did not intervene despite several calls to the emergency services. Police have, however, reportedly provided protection to some two hundred Roma who returned to the camp.[7]

The failure of police to protect Roma from violence and to investigate and prosecute incidents has been reported in a number of countries. As well, there have been many reports of police violence against Romani individuals and groups. In 2000 Amnesty International expressed its concern to Slovakian authorities about reported police operations carried out against entire Romani communities in response to suspected crimes committed by individual Roma. According to Amnesty International:

The common reported pattern which has emerged from all these incidents is of a dawn raid of massed police officers using dogs; restriction by the police of the freedom of movement of the Romani inhabitants; police officers uttering racist abuse; and ill-treatment or torture of members of the Romani community by the police officers.[8]

Political responses to the situation of the Roma have included incitement, active discrimination, denial, inaction, verbal condemnation and the implementation of remedial action. Miroslav Sladek, leader of the Republican Party in the Czech Republic, exemplified the first in 1998 when he stated that that the age of criminal responsibility for Roma should be lowered to birth, because their first crime is being born.[9]

One of the most blatant discriminatory acts occurred in the town of Usti nad Labem in the Czech Republic in 1999 when the local authority erected a concrete wall two metres high and 65 metres long to separate Roma and non-Roma residents. Czech government leaders, including President Havel, denounced the town's action and it was declared illegal. After a short period the wall was removed.[10] In Romania, Dr Dan Oprescu, the head of the government's National Bureau for Roma indicated the absence of political will to bring about change when he stated: 'There is certainly a degree of non-intervention and even complicity by the Government towards police brutality and mob violence against the Roma which is only the tip of the iceberg.'[11]

See also: **Apartheid, Ethnic cleansing, Genocide, Xenophobia**

'Queers'

First of all it was gonna be the blacks, then the Asians, then queers.

David Copeland, explaining why he had selected three particular sites in London to explode bombs in 1999.[1]

●　●　●

The first bomb set by David Copeland was in Brixton, where many black people live. The second was in East London, home to many people of Asian origin. The third was in the Admiral Duncan pub in Soho, central London, known as a gay venue. Copeland's bombs killed three people and injured 139. He was convicted of murder and was sentenced to imprisonment for life.

Copeland was an avowed admirer of Nazi Germany, where racism and homophobia were also ideologically linked and both given murderous expression. Shortly after coming to power, the Nazis banned all gay and lesbian organisations and established an 'Office for the Combating of Homosexuality and Abortion'. The government's hostility to homosexuality and abortion reflected its drive to increase the 'Aryan' population. Fifty thousand men are estimated to have been convicted as 'officially defined homosexuals' of whom between 5,000 and 15,000 were incarcerated in concentration camps. In the camps they were required to wear marks of various colours and shapes – including pink triangles – to distinguish them from other categories of prisoner. 'Many survivors have testified that men with pink triangles were often treated particularly severely by guards and inmates alike

Image on website of 'Blood and Honour', a racist group, 2001

because of widespread biases against homosexuals.'[2]

Homophobia continues to be common among racist groups, to some of which Copeland belonged. In the US and Europe, racist skinheads have violently attacked gays and lesbians. The US racist organisation Knights of the Ku Klux Klan complains about the betrayal of white citizens by 'the politicians of today (who) are the messed up kids of the 60s. They came from the homosexual, racemixing, Communist, anti-law and order, revolution'.[3]

In a rare moment of agreement with a black separatist organisation, the Klan was pleased to note that black Muslims also 'support separation and are opposed to race mixing and homosexuality'.[4] Offering his views on the fate of white people who did not leave post-apartheid South Africa, US black separatist Khalid Muhammad stated in 1993: 'We kill the women. We kill the babies. We kill the blind. We kill the cripples. We kill them all. We kill the faggot. We kill the lesbian.'[5]

The conjunction of racism and homophobia is a matter of interest in two respects: analysis and action. First, it suggests an interesting line of inquiry for those who want to understand the psychology of fear and

● Members of neo-fascist organisation, Forza Nuova, demonstrating against the hosting of World Pride, a gathering of lesbian, gay, bisexual and transgender people from around the world, in Rome, July 2000. The banner reads: 'Give the Colosseum to the gays? Only if the lions are in it.'

© AP

hate – why does 'difference' arouse such powerful antipathy? Second, it indicates a basis for co-operation between what are generally two distinct groups of activists, opponents of racism and of homophobia. The consequences of each group pursuing own interests, of failing to recognise shared concerns, may be great. In Nazi Germany, Reverend Martin Niemoller noted, the disunity of the targets of persecution created the opportunity for their destruction:

First they came for the communists, but I was not a communist – so I said nothing. Then they came for the social democrats, but I was not a social democrat – so I did nothing. Then came the trade unionists, but I was not a trade unionist. And then they came for the Jews – so I did little. Then when they came for me, there was no one left who could stand up for me.[6]

R
● ●

Rape

TO A WHITE GIRL
I hate you
Because you're white.
Your white meat
Is nightmare food.
White is

The skin of Evil.
You're my Moby Dick,
White Witch,
Symbol of the rope and
    hanging tree,
Of the burning cross.

I became a rapist... Rape was an insurrectionary act. It delighted me that I was defying and trampling upon the white man's law, upon his system of values, and that I was defiling his women – and this point, I believe, was the most satisfying to me because I was very resentful over the historical fact of how the white man has used the black woman. I felt I was getting revenge.

Eldridge Cleaver, 1960s black US activist who confessed to raping a number of white women.[1]

● ● ●

The Old Testament of the Bible specified two punishments for rape. If an Israelite man raped an Israelite virgin pledged to be married, the penalty was death. If she was not pledged to be married, he was required to pay her father fifty shekels (0.6 kilogram of silver) and marry her. However, if the woman was captured from the enemy following war, a man was entitled to do with her as he wished.

Captured women, children and livestock, the Bible instructed, 'you may take as plunder for yourselves. And you may use the plunder the Lord your God gives you from your enemies.'[2]

The Biblical link between rape and race is found throughout history and around the world: a man who raped a woman of his own community was subject to punishment but a man might rape a woman of another race as an act of war or a 'spoil' of war with impunity.

In the words of the United Nations Special Rapporteur [independent expert] on violence against women:

[rape in war is] a battle among men fought over the bodies of women. Sexual violence against women is meant to demonstrate victory over the men of the other group who have failed to protect their women. It is a message of castration and emasculation of the enemy group.[3]

During the last hundred years, rape has repeatedly been documented in internal and international conflicts throughout the world. The following cases are illustrative.

Dutch survivor Jan Ruff-O'Herve, surrounded by former sex slaves from the Philippines, Indonesia, Korea, Taiwan and China. They testified at a mock trial of Japan for World War II sexual slavery.

© Associated Press

China: During their conquest of Nanking in 1937, Japanese troops killed many civilians and raped many women. The episode became known internationally as 'The Rape of Nanking'. Subsequently, the Japanese military abducted women in Korea, China, the Philippines and Indonesia and forced them to serve as 'sex slaves' in military brothels.

Congo: Congolese forces raped Belgian women immediately after the country attained independence in 1960. Susan Brownmiller describes the rapes as 'acts of undifferentiated hostility of men toward women, perpetrated on nonbelligerents in the course of celebration, in this case a celebration of independence... with the raped women cast as symbol of the hated oppressor...'[4]

South Africa: A number of witnesses to an official inquiry into human rights violations during the apartheid period told of sexual violence being used to coerce and terrorise opponents of the regime. For example, Ms Thandi Shezi testified that she was detained by police who poured acid on her and choked her. She told the inquiry that one said:

We must just humiliate her and show her that this ANC [African National Congress, opponents of apartheid] can't do anything for

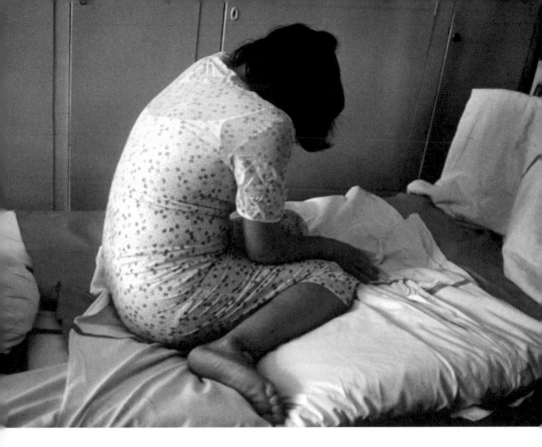

● An 18 year-old Bosnian Muslim woman recovers after aborting a pregnancy resulting from rape in 1992. During the war in the former Yugoslavia in that period, rape was used 'not only as an attack on the individual victim, but... to humiliate, shame, degrade and terrify the entire group. There are reliable reports of public rapes, for example, in front of the entire village, designed to terrorize the population and force ethnic groups to flee'.[6]

Nina Berman/Sipa Press

her' then the whole four of them started raping me whilst they were insulting me and using vulgar words and said I must tell them the truth.[5]

Rape under international law
In 1474 Peter van Hagenbach was tried before what has been described as the world's first international criminal court, in the town of Briesach, in what is now Germany. Hagenbach was an official of Duke Charles of Burgundy, who had instituted a reign of terror against the citizens of Breisach (then in the territory of the Archduke

of Austria) and neighbouring territories which Charles wanted to incorporate into his empire. A court of judges from Breisach and of other towns opposed to Charles, convicted Hagenbach of crimes including murder and rape, and sentenced him to death.[7]

Rape was implicitly or expressly prohibited in various laws of war and civil conflict that developed during subsequent centuries but rarely prosecuted. Following the Second World War, an international tribunal was established to prosecute people charged with crimes committed in Asia. It convicted two people in relation to the mass rape of women by Japanese troops in Nanking. Although rape had commonly occurred during the war in Europe as well, no one was prosecuted for it at the international tribunal for that region.

In 1998, Rwandan Jean Paul Akayesu was the first person to be convicted of the crime of genocide in which one of the constituent acts was rape. Akayesu, a town mayor, had encouraged Hutus to rape Tutsi women. Rape and sexual assault was committed against Tutsi women because they were Tutsi. 'Sexual violence was a step in the process of destruction of the Tutsi group – destruction of the spirit, of the will to live, and of life itself', the court found.[8]

Later that year, the International Criminal Tribunal for the former Yugoslavia convicted Hazim Delic of committing rape as the crime of torture. Delic was commander of a prison in which Bosnian Muslim and Croat forces detained Bosnian Serbs. Explaining its decision in relation to one of the victims, Grozdana Cecez, the court stated that the rapes were intended to coerce Ms Cecez to provide information about her husband, who was believed to be an armed rebel, and to punish her for her husband's acts. As well, the fact that the rapes were committed by an armed official in a prison camp, and were known to other staff and to the inmates, 'evidences Mr Delic's purpose of seeking to intimidate not only the victim but also other inmates, by creating an atmosphere of power and helplessness'.[9]

In the same case, Delic and another defendant, Zdravko Mucic, were convicted of 'inhuman treatment' and 'cruel treatment' with respect to a male prisoner who was forced to perform fellatio on another male prisoner. The court noted that the incident could also have been prosecuted as rape.

See also: **Ethnic cleansing, genocide**

Slavery

In 1987, when I was 10 years old, the Arab militia from the north came to our village. They killed the men – my grandfather was shot in front of my eyes – and took the children and women. We were taken to a northern town, Daien, and put in a big stockade. It was a slave market. A man named Ahmed Adam bought me. He made me herd his goats and do domestic work all day. If I wanted to rest, he threatened to kill me. I was there for 10 years.

When I grew older, Ahmed Adam would come at night and try to rape me. One night he threatened me with a knife and stabbed my right leg. I started running, with my leg bleeding. I found a truck taking cattle to Babanusa, and I hid with the cattle so the driver would not see me.

Abud Macam, from the Dinka people of Sudan, who was accepted as a refugee by the USA in 2000.[1]

Slavery has occurred throughout recorded history and in all regions of the world. It has taken many forms: following wars, the victors have enslaved the vanquished; weak nations have given slaves as tribute to powerful neighbours; women and girls have been sold for sex and for marriage; poverty has driven adults to sell themselves or their children; the children of slave women have been the property of slaveholders from the moment of their birth, as described in this

A VINDE

Un Prim Sálaş de Robi şau

SCLAVI ŢIGANEŞTI

Print o licitaţie la Amiaḑá a
. Mânăştire d. şt. *ELIAS*
la 8 mai *M.D.* CCC. L. II.

cine se compuná din 18 Omeni,
10 Bajaţi, 7 femei & 3 ffete
: in condiţie finá :

Grifo

● Poster advertising slave auction in Wallachia, Romania, 1852. It reads: 'For sale: a prime lot of Gypsy slaves, for sale by auction at the Monastery of St Elias, May 8, 1852. Consisting of eighteen men, ten boys, seven women and three girls, in fine condition.'[2]

account of by a former slave in 19th century USA.

I saw a mother lead seven children to the auction block. She knew that some of them would be taken from her, but they took all. The children were sold to a slave-trader, and their mother was bought by a man in her own town. Before night her children were all far away. She begged the trader to tell her where he intended to take them, this he refused to do. How could he, when he knew he would sell them,

●   Madhol, Sudan 1998. A group of freed slaves led by Ahmed, a 'slave retriever' working with anti-slavery organisation Christian Solidarity International. (www.iAbolish.com).

one by one, wherever he could command the highest price? I met that mother in the street, and her wild haggard face lies today in my mind. She wrung her hands in anguish, and exclaimed, 'Gone. All gone. Why don't God kill me?' I had no words wherewith to comfort her. Instances of this kind are of daily, yea, of hourly occurrence.[3]

In some countries – China, Korea and India among them – slaveholders and their slaves were drawn from the same groups. However, historians suggest that slaves were generally drawn from outside the national or religious group of the slaveholder – 'the Spanish could not enslave Spaniards, Arabs could not enslave Arabs, and Christians and Muslims could not enslave their coreligionists'.[4]

During the Middle Ages, international slave trading became a major activity within both Europe and the Islamic world and the sources of supply were diverse. The pagan Slavs of Central and Eastern Europe were victims of both Christians and Muslims and gave their name, Slav, to the practice, slavery.

The European colonisation of the Americas created a new demand for slaves. When the demand exceeded what could be obtained from among the indigenous people, slave traders looked to Africa. As many as 10 million West African slaves were landed in the Americas between the mid-15th century and the late 19th century.

Within Africa, black Africans were traders as well as victims. In the Americas, however, slaveholders were white and the difference was significant: slavery was justified on the grounds of racial superiority, an ideology that survived beyond the abolition of the institution. In the opinion of some scholars, the religious and pseudoscientific notions that defenders of slavery employed were no more than a cloak for the economic self-interest that was the real foundation of the practice. As one commentator has expressed it, 'racism was the consequence of slavery' rather than its cause.[5]

The trans-Atlantic slave trade was abolished throughout Europe by legislation following lengthy political agitation. Force rather than politics was required to abolish slaveholding in a number of countries. In the French Caribbean colony of Saint-Domingue, for example, slavery was abolished following a rebellion in 1791 led by freed slave Toussaint L'Ouverture. In the USA, slaves escaped along the so-called **underground railroad** to freedom in Canada and in states where slavery was prohibited, until the slaveholding states were defeated in a civil war and slavery abolished in 1865.

In the first part of the 20th century, international concern about the persistence of slavery in parts of Asia, Africa and the Middle East led to the adoption of a global treaty to abolish slave trading and slavery, the Slavery Convention of 1926. The Convention defined slavery quite narrowly, as 'the status or condition of a person over whom... the powers attaching to the right of ownership are exercised'. For the victims, however, the evil of slavery derives from the control that other people exercise over them, even if the controllers do not claim legal ownership. This was recognised in a supplementary slavery treaty of 1956 which extended the conduct that is prohibited to 'institutions and practices similar to slavery', including bonded labour (this occurs when a person pledges to provide personal services to another person for an unlimited period of time as security for a debt, and the nature of the services is not defined), forced marriage and child labour.

Slavery today

In recent decades, other practices that effectively enslave people have become prominent. They include, in particular, prostitution, the exploitation of immigrant workers and 'forced labour.'

Many thousands of women and children are abducted, tricked or sold into enforced prostitution within and between countries. Women from Eastern Europe have been sold to brothel operators in western Europe, the USA and Israel; girls from Nigeria have been trafficked to Italy; in their own countries, women from poor rural areas in Nepal, Bangladesh and India have been trafficked into the sex trade in major cities, as have children from the Amazon region in Brazil.

Reports of immigrant workers who have effectively been held captive by employers have come from a number of countries including the USA, the UK, France and Saudi Arabia. The areas of employment include farms, factories, hotels, and private households, and the means of control used by employers range from force to threatening to report illegal immigrants to the authorities.

Forced labour has been identified as a major practice in Myanmar [Burma]. Thousands of men, women and children in Myanmar have reportedly been forced by the military to work as labourers and bearers and on construction projects owned by the government; racial minorities in particular have been victimised.[6]

International slavery expert Kevin Bales estimates that there are as many as 27 million slaves in the world today, 'more…. than all the people stolen from Africa in the time of the transatlantic slave trade'.[7] By far the largest group comprises adult and child bonded labourers – up to 20 million – in India, Pakistan, Bangladesh and Nepal. A large proportion of India's bonded labourers are Dalits.[8]

Although prohibited by law, slavery continues in Mauritania and there is a distinct racial divide: the slaves are black Africans, the slaveholders (though not legally owners) are of Arab origin. A similar pattern of slaveholding has also been reported in the Sudan. But racially based slavery as in Mauritania is now exceptional, Bales suggests, as 'the criteria of enslavement today do not concern color, tribe, or religion; they focus on weakness, gullibility and deprivation'.[9]

See also: **Caste, Faith**

T

Truth

An old Balkan tale tells of a man leafing through one newspaper after another. 'Father, father, can I help you?' his son asks. 'No,' the man brushes the boy aside and continues skimming only the headlines of the papers. At last, he jabs his finger at one crumpled page and cries, 'Here it is! I knew it all along.' He throws the other papers on the floor and clings to his one headline. That the other papers contradict this story is irrelevant. He has found the Truth.

Julie Mertus, *Kosovo – How Myths and Truths Started a War*[1]

Julie Mertus wanted to document the 'factual truth' of the conflict between Serbs and ethnic Albanians in Kosovo. After two years research in Kosovo and Serbia, Mertus realised that she 'had it all wrong'. She said: 'For the most powerful diplomats, the facts could be crucial for determining and assessing blame and for taking action. The people of the region, however, pattern their behavior around what they believe to be true, based not on what some outside "expert" writes but on their own personal experiences and on the myths perpetuated by the local media and other popular storytellers.'[2]

In the event, then, what Mertus documented was how Serbian and Albanian perceptions shaped their interpretations of a number of incidents which fuelled the conflict between them. One such incident was the Martinović case.[3]

On 1 May 1985, Serb Djordje Martinović was admitted into

● Tulsa riot – 'The body of a dead Black Man is displayed out in the open for other Black men to view as they were "interned" at the convention center during the worst riot in US history.' [Black Holocaust Society]

hospital with serious internal injuries. According to Yugoslav newspaper reports, he had been attacked by two unknown Albanian men who forced a bottle into his rectum and left him, unconscious and bleeding. Public investigators issued a statement that Martinović had confessed that his wound was self-inflicted. Doctors provided conflicting opinions about whether or not Martinović could have inflicted the injury on himself.

Although what actually happened to Martinović was never authoritatively established, the case seriously inflamed long-standing tensions between Albanians and Serbs. Many Albanians believed that Martinović had lied about being attacked. Serbian commentators suggested that Martinović's confession had been coerced and that the alleged attack was part of an Albanian conspiracy to drive Serbs from Kosovo. A Serbian peace activist told Mertus: 'Since Martinović, whenever I hear of an Albanian accused of a crime, I think first he is guilty. I know this is not the right way, but I do.'[4]

The Martinović case, Mertus suggests, illustrates a universal phenomenon: 'We seek out the Truth that best fits our own notions of right and wrong, our idea of who is good and who is evil.'[5] Counter-parts of the Martinović case can be found throughout history and around the world.

The blood libel

On the eve of Easter, 1144, the body of a boy named William was found in a wood near the city of Norwich, England. He apparently died of natural causes, according to historian Cecil Roth, 'but the story soon spread that he had been put to death a day or two before by the Jews, in mockery of the Passion of Jesus, to celebrate their Passover feast'.[6] The belief that Jews murder children for ritual purposes spread to continental Europe with awful consequences. The same accusation was made against the Jews of Blois in France in a similar case in 1171, though there was no body as proof of the charge. Most of the community was executed by burning. By the close of the 15th century there were at least 50 more such attacks on Jewish communities.[7]

Over the centuries the so-called 'blood libel' was persistently revived in Europe and beyond. In 1840, Jews in Damascus were accused of the ritual murder of Father Thomas, Superior of the Franciscan religious community in the city, and his servant. Community leaders were arrested and tortured to secure confessions. A delegation of Jews from England and France obtained an audience with the Sultan of the Ottoman Empire who issued a decree acquitting the accused people and pronounced the charge a gross libel. The Damascus blood libel was recalled in 2000 in an article by Adil Hammuda in the semi-official Egyptian newspaper *al-Ahram* entitled 'A Jewish Matzah Made from Arab Blood'.[8] According to Hammuda: *The bestial drive to knead Passover matzah with the blood of non-Jews is found in the records of the Palestinian police where there are many recorded cases of Arab children who disappeared and were later found torn to pieces without a single drop of blood. The most reasonable explanation is that the blood was taken to be kneaded into the matzah dough of extremist Jews to use during Passover.*

The Tulsa riot

In Tulsa, Oklahoma on 30 May, 1921, Dick Rowland was alone in an elevator with the operator, Sarah Page. He was black and she was white. Sarah Page claimed that he attacked her. News of the alleged attack quickly spread in the white community – a **Ku Klux Klan** stronghold – and accounts of what supposedly occurred became exaggerated. A newspaper reported that Rowland had scratched Page's hands and face and torn her clothes. Police arrested Rowland and an armed white crowd surrounded the courthouse where he was detained. An armed black group came to protect him. On 1 June thousands of white rioters looted and burned the black area of the city. As many as 300 black people are estimated to have been killed.

Some days after the events the managing editor of the newspaper that reported the attack on Page admitted that 'the scratches and torn clothes were fictions'.[9] Walter White, an official of the National Association for the Advancement of Colored People, conducted an investigation and concluded that when Page – who was alone in the elevator – saw that it had been called for by a black man, she started the car before Rowland had completely entered. 'To save himself from injury, Rowland threw himself into the car, stepping on the girl's foot in doing so. Page screamed and, when a crowd gathered outside the elevator, claimed she had been attacked'.[10]

Rowland was released from jail two weeks after the riots and three months later Sarah Page dropped the charges and left Tulsa.

There is no compelling evidence that Djorje Martinović, William and Sarah Page were the victims of any crimes at all, much less crimes that demonstrated the criminality not only of the alleged perpetrators but of their races. Despite uncertainty about what had actually occurred, each 'crime' inflamed public anger and provided potent weapons for hatemongers. Uncertainty counted for little because each 'crime' confirmed what people already believed to be the truth – that 'they' are dangerous.

See also: **Genocide, Hate speech, Xenophobia, ZOG**

Underground railroad

With the coming of the Second World War, an imprisoned Europe turned hopefully or desperately toward the freedom of the Americas ... Lisbon became the great embarkation point but not everybody could get to Lisbon directly and so a tortuous roundabout refugee trail sprang up ... across the rim of Africa to Casablanca. Here the fortunate ones through money or influence or luck might obtain exit visas and scurry to Lisbon and from Lisbon to the New World, but the others wait in Casablanca. And wait. And wait...

The 1942 feature film *Casablanca* begins with these narrated words, setting the scene for a story about those seeking refuge and those who assist them.

In 1849, Harriet Tubman fled from her slavemaster in the state of Maryland to Pennsylvania, where slavery was prohibited. She returned to Maryland a year later and led her sister and two children to freedom. In the following years she made another 18 journeys into Maryland and helped more than 300 fugitive slaves to safety in states that did not permit slavery and to Canada, which did not extradite slaves. Slaveholders offered thousands of dollars reward for her capture.

Harriet Tubman was one of a number of 'conductors' on what became known as the 'underground railroad', with various routes and secret safe houses, called stations, along the route. Conductors included

A policeman patrolling the beach at Tarifa, southern Spain, 24 July 2000, passes the body of a young sub-Saharan who had attempted to reach Spain by sea.

© PA Photos/EPA

escaped slaves like Tubman, free black people, northern abolitionists and church leaders. It is estimated that as many as 100,000 slaves escaped the South, in defiance of punitive 'fugitive slave' laws and the efforts of slave hunters. Tubman was never caught and delivered all her 'passengers' safely.

More than a century later a new underground railroad called the 'sanctuary movement' was established in the USA. In the 1980s, the US government welcomed refugees from Communist-led regimes such as Cuba but was unsympathetic to those fleeing anti-Communist dictatorships supported by the US, such as those in Guatemala and El Salvador. In 1985, *Newsweek* reported: 'Of the 13,373 requests for asylum from Salvadoreans to the [Immigration and Naturalization Service] 323 were granted.'[1] The sanctuary movement emerged in response to the plight of the unwanted Central American asylum seekers, as Jim Corbett, one of the founders, explained:

On 4 May 1981, I heard about a Salvadoran refugee who had been caught by the Border Patrol. The following day I went looking for him. The day after that, having learned that refugees were pouring across the border but were being caught and returned by federal officials, my wife Pat and I set up an apartment for them in our home. It was soon jammed full. Assuming that life-and-death crises of this kind are always short-term emergencies, we held nothing in reserve, but in the course of the next few months we began to realize, as our energy and resources dwindled, that the emergency was chronic and the crisis in Central America may be no more than the beginning. Similar experiences were occurring in churches and homes throughout Mexico and along the length of the border.[2]

By 1984, despite criminal prosecutions of people involved, around 150 churches had declared themselves 'sanctuaries' which would seek to protect refugees from the authorities, while hundreds of congregations pledged their support. 'Church sanctuaries for refugees bear witness to the same moral values which inspired the underground railroad for escaped slaves,' the American Baptist Churches declared in 1985, and stated their commitment to assisting refugees despite being subject to prosecution.[3]

However, those who smuggled the refugees across the border from Mexico did so for money and were called 'coyotes'. Today, coyotes operate in every region of the world. They are called 'snakeheads' in China, *scafisti* in Albania and 'smugglers' by governments. They have eagerly seized the vast financial opportunity created by the fact that the number of people seeking to escape persecution and poverty far exceeds the number who are welcome in safe and wealthy countries. According to the US government, trafficking in people 'is one of the fastest growing and most lucrative criminal enterprises in the world', yielding profits of billions of dollars.[4] Only drugs and guns earn more money for organised crime.

Over the last decade, governments of many countries have sought to deter and block the arrival of refugees and unauthorised migrants by implementing a wide range of measures. They have erected fences at land borders and send armed boats to patrol coastal waters; they fine airline carriers and truck drivers who transport undocumented people; they imprison asylum-seekers or prohibit them from working to supplement meagre welfare allowances.

Still large numbers come, creating what one observer describes as 'an expensive game of wits being played along the frontiers of the rich world. It is a worldwide contest, in progress anywhere between the state of New Jersey and Taiwan; Queensland and New Mexico'.[5] For many refugees and migrants, the cost of losing the contest has been high. They have been deceived and robbed, raped and killed; they have drowned when their boats sank en route to Australia; they have suffocated in a truck travelling from the Netherlands to Britain; they have frozen to death in the Himalayan mountains, walking from Tibet to Nepal; they have died of thirst in the deserts straddling the US-Mexican border.

What becomes of the persecuted and the poor still seeking to escape when the smugglers are put out of business and underground railroads shut down? Many will remain trapped. Some will find their own way out and find a better place and some, like Yaguine Koita and Fode Tounkara, will fail. In 1999, the two 14-year-old boys hid in the undercarriage of a plane shortly before it left Guinea for Belgium. They froze to death.

Among the boys' meagre possessions a Belgian official found an envelope that said: 'In case we die...' It contained a note written by Yaguine Koita and Fode Tounkara, appealing to the 'Excellencies, Messrs. members and officials of Europe' to help the children of Africa. 'And if you see that we have sacrificed and risked our lives,' they wrote, 'it is because there is too much suffering in Africa and we need you to struggle against poverty and put an end to war in Africa.'[6]

Volk

Visions of race relations

Peoples of different races and religions should not mix…[O]nly if there is one race and one religion will our country be prosperous and peaceful.

Lieutenant General Myo Nyunt, Minister for Religious Affairs, Myanmar [Burma], 1995.[1]

● ● ●

Lieutenant General Myo Nyunt's recipe for national peace and prosperity is far from new. The virtues of racial homogeneity were strongly advocated by German nationalists in the 19th and 20th centuries. The central concept in their vision was *Volk*, German for 'a people' or 'nation'. Members of a *Volk* were believed to have a common historical and cultural background, sharing a mystical essence.

Volk was a racial notion. Jews, Roma and other groups were considered outsiders and threats to the welfare of the *Volk*. Adolf Hitler said that 'the basic ideas of the National-Socialist [Nazi] movement are *volkisch* and *volkisch* ideas are National-Socialist'. The Nazi regime translated the ideas into policies that included the expulsion and murder of people who were not members of the *Volk*.

Ethnic cleansing, genocide and **apartheid** are policies that have been used to transform racially diverse societies into homogenous ones. Immigration controls and laws against **miscegenation** are measures that have been used to prevent racial diversity occurring or increasing.

● Protest against proposals to repeal apartheid, South Africa 1990. The poster reads: 'Do you want your next door neighbour to look like this? All you have to do is vote NP [National Party]'.

The melting pot

Like *Volk*, the 'melting pot' vision of an ideal society is also one of homogeneity. But whereas the central characteristic of *Volk* is people united by shared ancestry, in the 'melting pot' society in which people of diverse origins have adopted a common culture and identity.

The term originated as the title of an early 20th-century play by Israel Zangwill, an emigrant to the USA. In the play, Zangwill transferred the story of Romeo and Juliet to the USA; their families became Russian Jews and Russian Cossacks, groups in conflict in their country of origin. Zangwill's message was that the old hatreds were no longer appropriate. Immigrants had to lose the identities of their origins and adopt a single new identity: Americans.

Governments have used a variety of measures to induce or force indigenous peoples, immigrants and other minorities to abandon their distinctive cultures. For example, after the Second World War, Japan adopted a policy of assimilation towards its substantial population of Korean origin. Koreans were, for example, required to take Japanese names and to speak Japanese in public.[2] In Botswana, the government has imposed severe restrictions on the hunting rights of 'Bushmen' and has reportedly attempted to drive Bushmen from a game reserve where many live.[3] The Bushmen depend on game for survival and hunting is central to their religion and culture. In 1997, Botswana's then Vice-President [now President] Festus Mogae remarked: 'How can you have a stone-age creature continue to exist in the time of computers? If the Bushmen want to survive, they must change, otherwise, like the dodo, they will perish.'[4]

Tossed salad

Assimilation policies around the world have had mixed success. Many people do consider themselves to have a single identity – they are American, Australian, Canadian, British and so forth. Other people describe themselves in terms of dual or hyphenated identities, combining ethnic or racial identity and nationality – they are, for example, Italo-American or Chinese Australian. The word 'multicultural' was coined to describe societies with groups that retain distinct identities but who are not socially and economically segregated, unlike apartheid. Some Canadians use the metaphor, 'tossed salad' to describe the mix.

In the late 20th century, the continued presence of distinct racial or ethnic groups, and political lobbying by them, persuaded a number of governments to change their policies from assimilation to what has been called 'multiculturalism'. This means that instead of seeking to destroy the existence of such groups, governments publicly welcome their presence and take account of their needs and concerns in various policies, such as recruitment of staff. According to Boston Police Commissioner Paul F Evans, 'having African-American and Hispanic and Vietnamese officers, people of different backgrounds and cultures who can conduct comfortable interviews with crime victims and can infiltrate crime rings that aren't white – I know the need for that is just common sense'.[5]

There is considerable controversy about whether the policy called multiculturalism is the most appropriate response to the demographic fact of diverse ethnic groups. Two of the major areas of disagreement are: first, to what extent groups should be entitled to freely practise their religions and express their cultures and second, whether multiculturalism promotes or reduces conflict.[6]

The first area of disagreement has involved issues such as 'dress codes' that conflict with cultural and religious practices. For example, in France, Muslim girls were excluded from school because they insisted on wearing headscarves and the authorities claimed the practice was inconsistent with the secular tradition of French education. In the UK Sikh men, whose religion requires them to wear turbans, sought exemption from having to wear helmets when riding motorcycles. Another contentious issue is whether polygamous marriages that are permitted under the law of another country from which immigrants have come should be lawful in the country in which they have settled.[7]

The second area of disagreement concerns the validity of Lieutenant General Myo Nyunt's belief cited on page 102, that racial homogeneity is essential for communal harmony. Opponents of multiculturalism focus on the dangers of conflict between racially or ethnically identified groups and point to the recurring wars and unrest in the former Yugoslavia since the early 1990s as evidence. Supporters of multiculturalism contend that conflict arises not out of diversity but out of discrimination and the suppression of people's religious and cultural practices.

National debates about policies toward racial and ethnic diversity are reflected at international level. In 1948, the authors of a draft of the international treaty on **genocide** proposed that the crime should include 'any deliberate act committed with the intent to destroy the language, religion or culture of a national, racial or religious group', for example by prohibiting the use of language or preventing a group using its own libraries and schools. The proposal divided countries and it was defeated after considerable debate.[8]

A different approach was evident in 1966, when nations adopted the International Covenant on Civil and Political Rights. This treaty states that countries with ethnic, religious or linguistic minorities must not deny people belonging to such minorities the right to enjoy their own culture, to practise their religion or to use their own language. In 1992, the United Nations General Assembly went significantly further when the member nations proclaimed the Declaration on the Rights of Persons Belonging to National or Ethnic, Religious and Linguistic Minorities. The Declaration states that governments should protect the existence and the ethnic, cultural, religious and linguistic identity of minorities and encourage conditions for the promotion of that identity.

See also: **Language, Xenophobia, Yellow Peril**

White Man's Burden

Take up the White Man's burden –
Send forth the best ye breed –
Go, bind your sons to exile
To serve your captives' need;
To wait, in heavy harness,
On fluttered folk and wild –
Your new-caught sullen peoples,
Half devil and half child.

From Rudyard Kipling's poem *The White Man's Burden*, February 1899.

When Kipling wrote *The White Man's Burden* the United States was at war with Spain and embroiled in a major debate between those who favoured and those who opposed its acquiring of colonies. The war ended soon after and Spain ceded Puerto Rico, Guam, and the Philippines to the USA and placed Cuba under US control. Kipling sent a copy of his poem to Theodore Roosevelt, who had led US forces against Spain in Cuba and was to become president in 1901.

The phrase 'the White Man's Burden' was seized upon by pro-imperialists to express the noble purpose served by the US in acquiring colonies. Anti-imperialists parodied the poem to suggest that self-interest rather than benevolence motivated US policy. A fine example is *The Brown Man's Burden* published shortly after Kipling's poem:

Pile on the brown man's burden
To gratify your greed;
Go, clear away the 'niggers'
Who progress would impede;
Be very stern, for truly
Tis useless to be mild
With new-caught, sullen people,
Half devil and half child.[1]

Having been raised in India, Kipling himself was not an uncritical admirer of the impact of colonialism on the 'new-caught' people. In 1895, he declined a request to endorse the missionary activity of the Presbyterian Church, stating:

It is my fortune to have been born and to a large extent brought up among those whom white men call 'heathen'; and ... it seems to me cruel that white men, whose governments are armed with the most murderous weapons known to science, should amaze and confound their fellow creatures with a doctrine of salvation imperfectly understood by themselves and a code of ethics foreign to the climate and instincts of those races whose most cherished customs they outrage and whose gods they insult.[2]

However, the notion that imperialism was undertaken for the benefit of the conquered was commonly asserted and had been so for centuries. In the mid-12th century, Pope Adrian IV authorised Henry II of England to take control of Ireland 'in order to extirpate the vices that have there taken root'.[3] The Spanish justified their conquest of the Americas as a divine mission, bringing Christianity to unbelievers and destroying societies whose inherent evil was demonstrated by practices such as human sacrifice. The French Empire, according to the French, reflected its *mission civilatrice* ('civilising mission'). Le Marechal Lyautey, Commissioner of a 1931 exposition on the French Empire, wrote: 'To colonize does not mean merely to construct wharves, factories, and railroads, it means also to instil a humane gentleness in the wild hearts of the savannah or the desert.'[4]

Perhaps the most audacious portrayal of imperialism as a humanitarian venture was that of King Leopold II of Belgium in the late 19th century.[5] Leopold envied the wealth and status that countries derived from their empires and determined to secure one for himself in

Black man's burden? A shooting party in Africa

© Mary Evans Picture Library

the vast area of Africa that had not yet been claimed by other European powers. He and Belgium were not motivated by self-interest, he assured those whose support he sought to enlist. On the contrary, '(t)o open to civilization the only part of our globe which it has not yet penetrated, to pierce the darkness which hangs over entire peoples, is, I dare say, a crusade worthy of this century of progress'.[6]

The territory King Leopold secured – now Democratic Republic of the Congo – was initially under his personal rule. The authorities, settlers and traders treated the indigenous peoples brutally and it is estimated that the population of the region was reduced by as many as 10 million. Leopold tried in vain to suppress the publication of reports about what was occurring and the cruel treatment of the Africans became the subject of a major international campaign.

Writer Joseph Conrad visited the Congo and set his novel *Heart of Darkness* there. The book's central character is Mr Kurtz, the agent of an ivory trading company. Kurtz is the author of a report to the 'International Society for the Suppression of Savage Customs', which ends with the chilling injunction 'Exterminate all the brutes!'.

"The White Man's Burden" illustrated by May, *Literary Digest*, 18 February, 1899

Mr Kurtz appears to have been modelled on people whom Conrad met or about whom he had heard. One likely model was policeman Leon Rom who is mentioned in a report of a speech to the Royal Statistical Society in 1898:

The Belgians have replaced the slavery they found by a system of servitude at least as objectionable. Of what certain Belgians can do in the way of barbarity Englishmen are painfully aware. Mr Courtney [Chairman of the Society] mentions an instance of Captain Rom, who ornamented his flower beds with heads of twenty-one natives killed in a punitive expedition. This is the Belgian idea of the most effectual method of promoting the civilization of the Congo.[7]

The horrific conduct of Captain Rom and others like him were not what British Prime Minister Margaret Thatcher had in mind nearly a century later, when she suggested that 'the story of how Europeans explored and colonised and – yes, without apology – civilised much of the world is an extraordinary tale of talent, skill and courage'.[8] Her speech was delivered in Belgium.

See also: **Imperialism**

Xenophobia

[T]he foreigner is not a very desirable person as a neighbour.
He first displaces the native and causes him to pay more rent.
He demoralises the Englishman's children by his filthy habits and
general disregard of decency and finally, as fast as the magistrates
improve the character of any district, the alien comes in, and with
him a host of prostitutes and criminals fleeing from justice abroad.

Frederick Bradshaw of the anti-immigrant British Brothers' League, 1904.[1]

Xenophobia: hatred or fear of foreigners or strangers or of their
politics or culture.[2] From Greek *xenos* – meaning strange, and *phobos*
– meaning fear. Any person can be a foreigner, branded by the colour
of their skin, accent, nationality, the food they eat or the place where
they worship. Some people, like Ana Bortz and Alberto Adriano, are
always foreigners.

Brazilian journalist Ana Bortz had lived in Hamamatsu City, Japan
for several years. In June 1998, while inspecting jewellery in a shop, she
was approached by the owner and asked to leave. A sign posted in the
shop banned foreigners. Bortz sued and became the first person to win
a racial discrimination case in Japan. The case attracted considerable
public attention. Bortz reported that she subsequently received
'hundreds of calls and letters from foreigners across Japan who say that
they have been ejected from shops or karaoke establishments or been

●   Racist UK group National Front march through Margate, Kent in a protest against immigration 8 April 2000.

subject to racial slurs while travelling on public transport'.[3]

Three young men kicked Alberto Adriano to death in Dessau, Germany in 2000. While kicking him, they shouted 'get out of our country, you nigger pig'. Adriano had migrated from Mozambique in 1980, spoke German, had a German wife and German nationality. However, to the men who attacked him he was a foreigner. He was also a foreigner to the media who reported his murder as the murder of 'a foreigner', an 'African' and 'a Mozambican'. One journalist reflected on the media coverage:

To most Germans, Adriano's death was extremely regrettable – a tragedy. But alien to many Germans is the concept that Adriano should never have been referred to as a foreigner.[4]

The definition of xenophobia cited above refers to hatred *or* fear. Often the emotions occur together: the foreigner is both feared *and* hated, perhaps for the same reasons. The threat of economic competition, real or imagined, is strongly felt by those whose livelihood is most precarious. People like Alice Mdakane, who sells vegetables on a street in Johannesburg, a city that has attracted many hawkers from other African countries:

Life is very difficult in South Africa. Why do these people want to come here and take our business? How are we going to feed our children? Do we go to their countries and steal their work? They should go home.[5]

In September 1998, 2,000 South African traders marched through the streets of the city, shouting 'Phansi nge makwerekere' ('Down with foreigners').[6]

Fear of the foreigner as criminal also arouses strong passions. In May 1999, 16-year-old Dutch girl Marianne Vaatstra was raped and murdered near the village of Kollum in the Netherlands. Suspicion fell on residents of a nearby centre for people seeking asylum and persisted despite the police announcing that they had investigated and cleared people seeking asylum as suspects. With considerable attention from the media, people from Kollum and the surrounding region quickly established a vigorous campaign to close the centre and oppose the establishment of new centres. Soon after, other villages announced their opposition to asylum-seeker centres.[7]

In April 2000, hundreds of residents of the Irish village of Clogheen attended a meeting to oppose the housing of 30 refugees in a local hotel. According to a media report, 'local woman, Rita Kiely, received huge applause when she said that the people deserved to know whether the refugees had criminal records, whether they were rapists, paedophiles or murderers.'[8] Earlier in the day part of the hotel was burnt out. Police said they were treating the fire as suspicious.

Community anxieties offer a tempting opportunity for politicians. In 1968, in a speech warning against the level of non-white immigration, British member of parliament Enoch Powell spoke of a letter he had received telling of an elderly person in his constituency who was the last white person living in her street:

She is becoming afraid to go out. Windows are broken. She finds excreta pushed through her letter box. When she goes to the shops, she is followed by children, charming wide-grinning piccaninnies. They

Paul Abayomi, victim of a racist attack, joins a protest against racist violence in Ireland, 2001. Almost 80 per cent of asylum-seekers responding to an Irish survey in 2000 reported that they had been the victims of racist taunts or unprovoked attacks.[10]

© Frank Miller, The Irish Times

cannot speak English, but one word they know. 'Racialist,' they chant.[9]

Powell did not name her and journalists and researchers were unable to discover who she was or indeed whether she existed at all. Anne Dummet, a race relations worker, noted that she had heard a similar anecdote about an old woman who was said to live in London. Apart from her place of residence, 'almost every circumstantial detail was the same'.[11] Powell's constituent must have been one of 'a large unhappy European family of the persecuted and righteously embittered', according to the British writer Nicholas Fraser, because they also appear in the speeches of other anti-immigration politicians, such as Jörg Haider of Austria and Jean Marie Le Pen of France.[12]

The language of xenophobia is often crude. In 1998, people from eastern Europe claiming asylum in Dover were described by a local newspaper as 'human sewage'.[13] Senior British police officers in 2001 noted that 'racist expressions towards asylum seekers appear to have become common currency and "acceptable" in a way which would never be tolerated towards any other minority group'.[14]

Politicians, journalists and other commentators refer to immigrants and to people seeking asylum in cataclysmic terms. The influx is said to be a 'flood' or an 'invasion'. 'Fortress Europe' is used to describe the aim of European government policies to restrict the numbers of migrants and refugees.

The language of xenophobia is often violent. Violence can come from any quarter. Reports of police ill-treatment of foreign nationals in France, Italy and other countries have been received by human rights organisations, as illustrated by this Amnesty International note on Austria in 2000:

A large majority of allegations [of ill treatment by police] comes from non-Caucasian Austrians and foreign nationals. Most report that they have been subjected to repeated kicks, punches, kneeing, beatings with truncheons and spraying with pepper after being restrained ... Police officers are also alleged to have used racist language in some instances.[15]

The language of xenophobia is often silent: hostile stares and suspicious glances; letters of rejection for job applications; apartments that have been 'let' just before the foreigner came to have a look. It is also embodied in laws that prevent asylum-seekers and immigrants from entering the country; laws restricting the employment that foreigners can undertake; laws that make it extraordinarily difficult to obtain citizenship.

See also: **Hate speech, Ku Klux Klan, Truth, Yellow Peril**

Yellow Peril

I believe we are in danger of being swamped by Asians... They have their own culture and religion, form ghettos and do not assimilate. Of course, I will be called racist but, if I can invite whom I want to my home, then I should have the right to have a say in who comes into my country.

Pauline Hanson, first speech as member of the Australian parliament, 10 September 1996.

● ● ●

Pauline Hanson expressed fears about Asian people that have been a major feature of Australian public and private life for more than 150 years. She was indeed widely condemned as a racist, as she had anticipated. A hundred years earlier, however, her sentiments would have been quite unremarkable in Australia and in a number of other countries ruled by people of European origin.

'Chink, don't let the sun set on your face in this town.' So read an 1889 sign posted at the entrance to a town in East Kootenay, British Columbia, warning Chinese immigrants not to entertain ideas of settling. *The Chink*, a poem published anonymously in a popular newspaper in Canada in 1901, captures some of the reasons for white hostility to Chinese immigrants:

Alas! Alas! 'tis sad to think
A white man pleads for a heathen Chink.
Does he think of the way he does his work,

Of the gruesome germs that around him lurk,
Wants him to cook the food he eats,
Wash his shirts and iron his sheets;
How he moistens his clothes and sprinkles the buns
With the water that washes his leprous gums;
Does he think of the loathsome opium den,
Where he sinks to the lowest grade of men.
Alas for the one who cannot find
A help among our white mankind.[1]

Attitudes towards Asians in domestic policies

From 1871 until 1947, Canada used tax as a means of discouraging Chinese immigration. The provincial government of British Columbia proposed additional measures including a law limiting the length of hair of men employed on public works: the length was shorter than the 'queues' or ponytails that many Chinese men wore.

During the 19th century, US federal, state and local governments legislated to deny people of Chinese origin citizenship and prohibited them from voting, testifying against white people, attending school with white children and marrying white people. From 1882, the US Congress passed a series of laws to restrict Chinese immigration and in 1917 immigration from almost all Asian countries was barred. The exclusion of Chinese immigrants was repealed in 1943 only after the US and China became allies in the war against Japan.

Australian colonies in the 19th century also imposed measures to restrict Chinese immigration. When they federated and became an independent country in 1901, the new national government immediately adopted what was commonly described as the 'White Australia' policy. The policy was eased in the 1960s and race was dropped as a criterion for the selection of immigrants in 1973. However, considerable opposition to Asian immigration remains. Asian immigrants and Australians of Asian background have often been the targets of racist attacks.

While Australia was in the process of removing barriers to Asian immigration, Britain imposed them. During the early 20th century the British brought thousands of labourers from India to build a railway in the colony that became Kenya. Thousands followed and settled. When Kenya became independent in 1963, its Asian residents, mainly of Indian origin, were offered a choice between Kenyan citizenship and

'The Mongolian Octopus – the grip on Australia' in popular Australian magazine *The Bulletin*, 21 August 1886.

retaining citizenship of the UK or that of another country. Many opted to retain UK citizenship as a safeguard in case they were forced to leave. Soon after, the Kenyan government implemented restrictions on non-citizens and Asians began to leave the country.

Faced with growing political and public opposition to the arrival of Kenyan Asians and to non-white immigration generally, the British government found itself in a dilemma. Government Minister Richard Crossman recorded in his diary for 19 October 1967 a meeting of the government's committee on immigration issues:

There are some 200,000 [Kenyan Asians with British passports] who are now threatened as a result of the black-Africa policy ... It's quite clear we couldn't allow some 50,000 Asians from Kenya to pour into Britain each year. On the other hand it's doubtful whether we have any legal or constitutional right to deny entry to these people from Kenya since they have British passports... We finally agreed that [the

117

immigration minister Roy Jenkins] must of course face the possibility
of this threat developing into reality and that he must work out
appropriate policies and consider the practicability of legislation.²

The government resolved the dilemma by rushing a law through
Parliament that allowed it to restrict immigration by Asians holding UK
passports. The assurance given to Asians choosing UK citizenship was
broken. *The Times* newspaper of 27 February 1968 described the
legislation as 'probably the most shameful measure' that the government
had asked its members in the Parliament to support.

Attitudes towards Asians in international relations

At the turn of the 20th century, whites came to fear not only Asian
immigrants, but also the potential power of Asian states and in
particular China and Japan. It was a fear that was given the name
'yellow peril', apparently by German Kaiser Wilhelm II, in ironic
circumstances. The event that inspired it was a revolt against European
imperialism in China.

The revolt was the Boxer Rebellion of 1899-1901, so called
because it was led by a group known as 'Righteous and Harmonious
Fists' who practised boxing and other athletic activities. The Boxers
wanted to drive foreigners from China. However, a military force from
Germany, Britain, France, the Austro-Hungarian Empire, the USA,
Russia, Japan and Italy crushed the rebellion and imposed harsh terms
on China. Despite China's weakness at the time, foreign observers
noted well the strength of the rebellion and the potential of the
country's large population if it was well organised. Japan's growing
power was also noted. Kaiser Wilhelm II was convinced that a great
'final' battle between the white and yellow races was imminent and the
white race must prepare for it.

In the event, the war of the races predicted by the Kaiser and
others did not happen, at least not as they had envisaged. The two
world wars of the 20th century began as conflicts between groups of
European countries and in both Japan was allied to one of the groups.

See also: **On the Origin of Species, Xenophobia**

ZOG

...let us leave our desks and go out wasting the multi-culti, multi-criminal ZOG inferno. There are comrades out ther (sic) right now in Britain and Ireland, in Germany and Poland, in Slovakia and Hungary, in the Czech Republic and Slovenia, in Croatia and Sebia (sic), in Denmark and Sweden, in Norway and Finland, in America and Australia – giving their everything so the Aryan race will live on. Let's give them a resolute, hard-hitting, helping hand in our common battle for a Whiter and brighter world – WHATEVER IT TAKES!

Statement of international racist groups network, 'Blood and Honour'.[1]

• • •

'ZOG' is an acronym for 'Zionist Occupation Government', a term used by various racist groups to describe an apparently independent government that is [so they believe] actually under the secret control of Jews. In the words of one such group, ZOG is 'the assortment of traitors and Zionist lackeys who control most of the White nations on this planet'.[2]

The term ZOG was apparently coined by US racist William Pierce. Under the pseudonym 'Andrew McDonald', Pierce wrote a novel *The Turner Diaries* in which 'Aryans' violently overthrow the US government and systematically kill Jews (who control the government), non-whites, communists, gays, and people who 'defiled their race' by marrying or living with blacks, Jews and 'other non-Whites'.

Image on website of racist group 'Blood and Honour', 2001

The belief that Jews secretly control or conspire to control the world is a very old anti-Semitic fantasy. The most notorious version is contained in a document entitled *The Protocols of the Elders of Zion* (sometimes translated as *Wise Men of Zion*) that purports to be an authentic record of a Jewish conspiracy. The document was apparently concocted by the Okhrana, the Russian secret service, in the late 19th century.[3] Although exposed as a forgery in 1920 it was translated and widely sold throughout Europe and elsewhere. To Adolf Hitler, *The Protocols* demonstrated 'with a truly horrifying certainty, the nature and the activity of the Jewish people and expose them in their inner connection as well as in their ultimate final aims'.[4] *The Protocols of the Elders of Zion* continues to be widely published in various languages including Arabic and Japanese. William Pierce is one of its US distributors.[5]

For many present day anti-Semites, compelling 'proof' of a powerful Jewish conspiracy is provided by the 'myth' that Nazi

Germany aimed to exterminate the Jews. According to Robert Faurisson, one of the leading advocates of this view: 'The alleged Hitlerian gas chambers and the alleged genocide of the Jews form one and the same historical lie, which permitted a gigantic financial swindle whose chief beneficiaries have been the state of Israel and international Zionism, and whose main victims have been the German people and the Palestinian people as a whole.'[6]

The titles of books by other proponents of this view clearly indicate the perspective: *Did Six Million Really Die?* by Richard Verrall, former leader of British neo-nazi National Front; *The Hoax of the 20th Century: the case against the presumed extermination of European Jewry* by US author Arthur Butz; *Great Lie of the 20th Century* by Swiss former school teacher Jürgen Graf; *Mit holocausti* ('The Myth of the Holocaust') published by the Polish political party Narodowe Odrozenie Polski, National Revival of Poland.

In 2000 British historian David Irving sued Professor Deborah Lipstadt for libel. She had described him as a 'Holocaust denier' who had deliberately manipulated and distorted evidence to conform with his 'ideological leanings and political agenda'. After a trial lasting three months, the judge found in favour of Professor Lipstadt. In his judgement, Mr Justice Gray stated:

The charges which I have found to be substantially true include the charges that Irving has for his own ideological reasons persistently and deliberately misrepresented and manipulated historical evidence; that for the same reasons he has portrayed Hitler in an unwarrantedly favourable light, principally in relation to his attitude towards and responsibility for the treatment of the Jews; that he is an active Holocaust denier; that he is anti-semitic and racist and that he associates with right-wing extremists who promote neo-Nazism.[7]

See also: **Genocide, Hate Speech, Miscegenation**

Sources

Books etc

Ellis Cashmore ed., *Dictionary of Race and Ethnic Relations*, Routledge, London. 1996.

Sandra Coliver ed., *Striking a Balance: Hate Speech, Freedom of Expression and Non-Discrimination*, Article 19, London. 1992.

Norman Duncan and Cheryl de la Rey, 'Racism: A Psychological Perspective', research paper for the National Conference on Racism, South Africa. 2000. sahrc.org.za/research-paper. 24 July 2001.

Nicholas Fraser, *The Voice of Modern Hatred – Encounters with Europe's New Right*, Picador, London. 2000.

Robert Jay Lifton, *The Nazi Doctors: A Study in the Psychology of Evil*, Macmillan, London. 1986.

Kenan Malik, *The Meaning of Race*, Macmillan, London. 1996.

Albert Memmi, *Racism*, University of Minnesota Press, Minneapolis. 2000.

World Directory of Minorities, Minority Rights Group International, London. 1997.

The Persistence and Mutation of Racism, International Council on Human Rights Policy, Geneva. 2000. www.ichrp.org

Geoffrey Robertson, *Crimes Against Humanity*, Penguin, London. 2000.

Searchlight, international anti-fascist magazine, PO Box 1576, Ilford IG5 0NG, UK. www.searchlightmagazine.com

Electronic information sources

I CARE: Internet Centre Anti-Racism Europe, http://wwwmagenta.nl/crosspoint/

www.hri.ca/racism

Anti-Racism Information Service. http://www.antiracism-infor.org

Organisations

Anti-Slavery International, Thomas Clarkson House, The Stableyard, Broomgrove Road, London SW9 9TL, UK. http://www.antislavery.org

European Monitoring Centre on Racism and Xenophobia, Rahlgasse 3, 1060 Vienna, Austria. http://eumc.at

Human Rights Watch, 350 Fifth Avenue, 34th Floor, New York, NY 10118-3299. http://www.hrw.org

Minority Rights Group International, 379 Brixton Road, London SW9 7DE UK. http://www.minorityrights.org

South Asia Human Rights Documentation Centre, B-6/6 Safdarjang Enclave Extension, New Delhi 110029, India. www.hrdc.net/shrdc/

Survival International, 11-15 Emerald Street, London WC1N 3QL, UK. www.survival-international.org

Southern Poverty Law Center. http://www.splcenter.org

Institute of Race Relations, 2-6 Leeke Street, King's Cross Road, London WC1X 9HS, UK. www.irr.org.uk/

Minorities at Risk Project, Center for International Development and Conflict Management, 0145 Tydings Hall, University of Maryland, College Park MD. 20742-7231 USA. http://www.bsos.umd.edu/cidcm/mar

United Nations. http://www.unhchr.ch. See in particular the Committee on the Elimination of Racial Discrimination and the Special Rapporteur on Contemporary Forms of Racism, Racial Discrimination, Xenophobia, and Related Intolerance

Endnotes

Introduction

1 *Zlata's Diary*, translated by Christina Pribichevic-Zoric, Chivers, Bath. 1994.
2 Natalie Angier, 'Do Races Differ? Not Really, DNA Shows', *The New York Times*. 22 August 2000.
3 *Here for Good – Western Europe's New Ethnic Minorities*, Pluto Press, London. 1984.
4 *The Cultivation of Hatred*, New York, W W Norton and Company, 1998.
5 Frances E Aboud and Anna Beth Doyle, 'Does Talk of Race Foster Prejudice or Tolerance in Children?', http://www.cpa.ca/cjbsnew/1996/ful_aboud.html.
6 *Racism*, University of Minnesota Press, Minneapolis. 2000.
7 Anthony Lewis, 'Ripple of Hope', *The New York Times*, 23 June 2001.

A

1 David Harrison, *The White Tribe of Africa*, BBC, London. 1981.
2 Paul Salopek, 'Some Afrikaners, in a twist, now seek their own homeland', *Chicago Tribune*. 16 March 2000.
3 Final Report of the Truth and Reconciliation Commission, Volume Five, Chapter One.
4 Phil Reeves, 'Israeli court gives Arabs historic right to buy land', *The Independent*. 9 March 2000.
5 Chin Ung Ho, *The Chinese of South-East Asia*, Minority Rights Group International, London. 2000.
6 Jerome Lewis, *The Batwa Pygmies of the Great Lakes Region*, Minority Rights Group International, London. 2000.
7 Reports submitted to Commission on Human Rights, UN Index E/CN.4/1996/72, Add.1, 23 January 1995 and E/CN.4/2000/16, 10 February 2000.

B

1 Jeffrey Rosen and Charles Lane, 'The Sources of the Bell Curve', Steven Fraser ed., *The Bell Curve Wars*, Basic Books, New York. 1995.
2 David Hume, *Of National Characters* (1753) cited in Patrick Richardson, *Empire and Slavery*, Longmans Green, London. 1968.
3 *The Mismeasure of Man*, Penguin, London. 1996.
4 *Ibid*.
5 'Aryan' – people supposedly descended from an Indo-European group. Michael Banton, 'Aryan', Ellis Cashmore, *Dictionary of Race and Ethnic Relations*, Routledge, London. 1996.
6 Adolf Hitler, *Mein Kampf*, cited in Lucy S Davidowicz, *The War Against the Jews 1933-45*, Penguin Books, London. 1990.
7 *The Preventable Genocide: Report of the International Panel of Eminent Personalities to Investigate the 1994 Genocide in Rwanda and the Surrounding Events*, www.oau.org/Document/ipep/report/rwanda. 13 January 2001.

8 Testimony of 'Witness V', International Criminal Tribunal for Rwanda, The Prosecutor versus Jean-Paul Akayesu, Case No. OCTR-96-4-T, Decision of 2 September 1998, Judgement, Paragraph 168.
9 Stephen Jay Gould, op cit.
10 UNESCO Statement on Race and Racial Prejudice, Paris. September 1967.
11 See, for example, Steven Fraser ed., *The Bell Curve Wars*, op cit.
12 'Celera Genomics Publishes First Analysis of Human Genome,' www.applera.com/press/prccorp021201.html. 31 May 2001.
13 Mark Henderson, 'Colour irrelevant, say genome researchers', *Daily Telegraph*. 12 February 2001.

C

1 Human Rights Watch, *Broken People – Caste Violence Against India's 'Untouchables'*, Human Rights Watch, New York. 1999.
2 'Untouched', *The Guardian*, 11 January 2001.
3 R Eugene Culas, 'Defending Dalit Rights in India', unpublished paper, 2000.
4 *Ibid*.
5 Smita Narula, *Entrenched Discrimination – the Case of India's 'Untouchables'*, International Council on Human Rights Policy, Geneva. 1999.
6 UN Committee on the Elimination of Racial Discrimination (CERD), Concluding observations of CERD on India Report 1996, CERD/C/304/ADD.13. 17 September 1996.
7 'A dalit goes to court', *The Hindu*, 13 June and 11 July 1999.
8 Human Rights Watch, op cit.
9 Annual report of the National Commission for Scheduled Castes and Scheduled Tribes, *Times of India*, February 1998, reported in Amnesty International, *Persecuted for challenging injustice – Human Rights Defenders in India*, AI Index ASA 20/08/00.
10 *Persecuted for challenging injustice*, op cit.
11 Report submitted by the Government of Nepal to the Committee on the Elimination of Racial Discrimination, UN document CERD/C/337/Add.4. 12 May 1999.
12 Simon Rawles, 'Bad Blood', *The Independent on Sunday*. 11 February 2001.

D

1 Rachel Swarms, 'Heard the one about the black South African comic and the white audience?' *The Observer*. 14 January 2001.
2 http://www.aclu.org/profiling/tales/index.html. 5 July 2001.
3 Peter Verniero and Paul H Zoubek, *Interim Report of the State Police Review Team Regarding Allegations of Racial Profiling*, 20 April 1999.
4 *Ibid* 7.

5 Letter from Texas Defender Service to Governor George W Bush, 3 August 2000; jury selection manual written by Assistant District Attorney John Sparling, 1969.

6 Amnesty International, *Killing with Prejudice: Race and the Death Penalty*, AI Index: AMR 51/52/99, May 1999.

7 *The Death Penalty in Black and White*, 1998. www.essential.org/dpic.

8 *Black Power: The Politics of Liberation in America*, Penguin, London. 1967.

9 *The Stephen Lawrence Inquiry – Report of an Inquiry by Sir William Macpherson of Cluny*, The Stationery Office, London. 1999.

10 *Ibid*.

11 Vikram Dodd, "'Malicious racism" in youth prison', *The Guardian*. 22 January 2001. Martin Narey, reported in Clare Dyer, 'Inquiry to examine racism in prisons', *The Guardian*, 18 November 2000.

12 *Black Power*, op cit.

E

1 Carl Sandburg, *Abraham Lincoln: The War Years*, volume 1, Harcourt Brace, New York. 1939.

2 For the origins of the term, see William Safire, 'Ethnic cleansing: clean words mask dirty deeds', http://www.bosnet.org/archive/bosnet.w3archive/9303/msg00082.

3 Michael Dugan and Josef Szwarc, '*There Goes the Neighbourhood!*' Macmillan, Melbourne. 1994.

4 Tony Kushner and Katharine Knox, *Refugees in an Age of Genocide*, Frank Cass, London. 1999.

5 Tadeusz Mazowiecki, Special Rapporteur of the Commission on Human Rights, in *The Situation of Human Rights in the Territory of the former Yugoslavia*, A/48/92, S/25341. 26 February 1993.

6 Roger Cohen, 'Ethnic Cleansing', in Roy Gutman and David Rieff eds, *Crimes Of War: What the Public Should Know*, Norton, New York. 1999.

7 High Commissioner on National Minorities, Organisation for Security and Co-operation in Europe, *Report on the Roma and Sinti in the OSCE Area*, The Hague, 2000.

8 Frank Newman and David Weissbrodt, *International Human Rights*, Anderson, Cincinnati. 1990.

F

1 Rev. Dr. Richard Furman's *EXPOSITION of the Views of the Baptists, Relative to the Coloured Population in the United States in a Communication to the Governor of South-Carolina*, Second Edition, 1838. http://www.furman.edu/~benson/docs/rcd-fmn1.htm. 5 July 2001.

2 Addressing the Millennium World Peace Summit of Religious and Spiritual Leaders held in 2000, http://www.milleniumpeacesummit.org/. 5 July 2001.

3 Bull *Romanus Pontifex*, 8 January, 1455.

4 *Christianity – A Global History*, Allen Lane, The Penguin Press, London. 2000.

5 *Ibid*.

6 Rosa Parks, *Quiet Strength*, Zondervan, Grand Rapids. 1994.

7 'Letter from Birmingham Jail', 16 April 1963, http://www.stanford.edu/group/King/frequentdocs/birmingham.pdf. 5 July 2001.

8 John Cornwell, *Hitler's Pope –The Secret History of Pius XII*, Viking, London, 1999, 280.

9 *Ibid*.

10 Misha Glenny, *The Balkans 1804-1999*, Granta, London. 1999.

11 Helen Fein, *Accounting for Genocide*, The Free Press, New York. 1979.

12 *The Preventable Genocide,* op cit (B note 7).

13 *Ibid*.

G

1 Bartolomé de Las Casas, *A Short Account of the Destruction of the Indies*, translated by Nigel Griffin, Harmondsworth, Penguin, 1992.

2 David E Stannard, *American Holocaust: Columbus and the Conquest of the New World*, New York, Oxford University Press. 1992.

3 Raphael Lemkin, 'Genocide – A Modern Crime', *Free World*, volume 4 (April 1945). http://www.preventgenocide.org/genocide/freeworld.htm. 5 July 2001.

4 *Bringing Them Home – National Inquiry into the Separation of Aboriginal and Torres Strait Islander Children from Their Families*, Commonwealth of Australia, 1997.

5 Survival International, *Disinherited – Indians in Brazil*, London, 2000.

6 Norman Lewis, 'Genocide', *Sunday Times*. 23 February 1969.

7 Commission for Historical Clarification, *Guatemala – Memory of Silence*, http://hrdata.aaas.org/ceh/report.html.

8 *Iraq's crime of genocide – The Anfal Campaign against the Kurds*. www.hrw.org/hrw/pubweb/Webcat-53.htm. 24 July 2001.

9 Sydney Schanberg, "Cambodia", *Crimes of War* op cit (E, note 6)

H

1 'Individual Responsibility of Defendants – Julius Streicher', *Nazi Conspiracy and Aggression*, Volume II, USGPO, Washington. 1946. http://www.ess.uwe.ac.uk/genocide/Streicher.htm. 5 July 2001.

2 Leo Kuper, *Genocide*, Yale University Press. 1981.

3 'Individual Responsibility of Defendants – Julius Streicher', op cit.

4 International Criminal Tribunal for Rwanda, Case number ICTR-97-32-I.

5 R v Keegstra [1990] 3 SCR.

6 Frank Collin and the National Socialist Party of America v Albert Smith and others, US Court of Appeals for the Seventh Circuit, 578 F.2d 1197.

I

1 Margherita G. Sarfatti, *Dux: Una Vita di Benito Mussolini*, translated by Frederic Whyte, Thornton Butterworth, London. 1925.

2 EHM Gorges, *Report on the Natives of South-West*

Africa and Their Treatment by Germany, London. 1918. Cited in Mark Cocker, *Rivers of Blood, Rivers of Gold – Europe's Conflict with Tribal Peoples*, Pimlico, London. 1999.

3 Cited in the Australian High Court, Mabo and others v Queensland (No.2) (1992) 175 CLR 1 F.C. 92/914.

4 AG Harper, 'Canada's Indian Administration: Basic Concepts and Objectives', *America Indigena*, 5, Number 2, April 1945), 127, cited in JR Miller, 'The State, the Church, and Residential Schools in Canada', 1999. http://anglican.ca/ministry/rs/resources/miller. 6 July 2001.

5 Phillip Wearne, *Return of the Indian*, Cassell, London. 1996.

6 Robert Macdonald, *The Maori of Aotearoa-New Zealand*, Minority Rights Group International, London. 1990.

7 Wearne, op cit.

8 *Ibid.*

9 Survival International, *Disinherited – Indians in Brazil*, London. 2000.

10 Wearne, op cit.

J

1 Betty Schechter, *The Dreyfus Affair*, Victor Gollancz, London. 1967.

2 Brian Barry, *Culture and Equality – An Egalitarian Critique of Multiculturalism*, Polity, Cambridge. 2001.

3 Charles Peguy, cited in Betty Schechter, op cit.

K

1 http://www.kukluxklan.org/faq.htm.

2 The Southern Poverty Law Center estimates that there are around 450 'active hate groups' in the USA. http://www.splcenter.org/intelligenceproject.

3 http://www.splcenter.org/legalaction.

4 The legality of this intervention was extremely controversial because it was not authorised by the United Nations, eg see Independent International Commission on Kosovo, www.kosovocommission.org/reports/10-law.

L

1 Randy Fred in Celia Haig-Brown, *Resistance and Renewal: Surviving the Indian Residential School* (Vancouver: Tillacum Library, 1988), cited in *Report of the Aboriginal Justice Inquiry of Manitoba, volume 1: The Justice System and Aboriginal People*, Province of Manitoba. 1991.

2 Wynford Vaughan-Thomas, *Wales: A History*, Michael Joseph, London. 1985.

3 Peter Sager, *Wales*, Pallas Guides, Athene, London 1991.

4 *ibid.*

5 David Bell, 'Lingua populi, lingua dei: Language, religion, and the origins of French revolutionary nationalism', *The American Historical Review*, vol C, no.5, December 1995.

6 *Bulletin de l'Enseignement en* AOF, No 45, 1921, cited in *Education in French colonies and former colonies*, Encyclopaedia Brittanica Online.

7 'Basque writer leaps into translation', UNESCO *Courier*, April 2000.

8 Amnesty International, *Bulgaria – Imprisonment of Ethnic Turks*. AI Index EUR/15/03/86, April 1986.

9 'Turkish PM softens line on Kurdish broadcast ban', CNN.com, 14 November 2000.

10 John Milloy, 'When a language dies', *Index on Censorship* 4. 1999.

11 Mwangi wa Mutahi, 'The trials of a Gikuyu writer', UNESCO *Courier*, April 2000.

12 *The Other Side of Eden*, Faber and Faber, London. 2001.

13 *Ibid.*

M

1 *Cobbett's Weekly Political Register*, 16 June 1804.

2 Cited in US Supreme Court decision, Loving v Virginia, 388 US 1, 1967.

3 *Ibid.*

4 Sidney Kaplan, 'Miscegenation', *Journal of Negro History*. June 1949.

5 Matt Kelley, 'South Africa's Hated Laws – the Prohibition of Mixed Marriages Acts', Mavin.net v1_laws.html.

6 *Kangura*, 10 December 1990, cited in African Rights, *Rwanda: Death, Despair and Defiance*, London. 1995.

7 Erik Kirschbaum, 'German extremists jailed as far-right crime surges', Reuters. 7 February 2001.

8 *Ibid.*

9 *The Observer*. 17 December 2000.

10 Mark Kromer, *Nation*. 19 February 2001.

N

1 Harpinder Kaur, *Gandhi's Concept of Civil Disobedience*, Intellectual Publishing House, New Delhi, 1986.

2 *Ibid.*

3 *Ibid.*

4 *The Words of Martin Luther King Jr*, Fount Paperbacks, London. 1985.

5 Malcolm X, *By Any Means Necessary*, Pathfinder, New York. 1992.

6 Mandela's statement to the Court, 20 April 1964. *Nelson Mandela – The Struggle Is My Life*, International Defence and Aid Fund for South Africa, London, no date.

O

1 A Desmond and J Moore, *Darwin*, Penguin Books, London, 1992.

2 *On the Origin of Species*, 6th Edition, Chapter IV.

3 Sven Lindqvist, *Exterminate all the Brutes*, Granta, London. 1998.

4 'The Human Genome and Our View of Ourselves', *Science magazine*, www.sciencemag.org/cgi/content/full/291/5507/1219.

5 *The Descent of Man*, 2nd Edition. 1874.

6 'International relations', Encyclopaedia Brittanica Online.

7 Ingrid A Kircher, *The Kanaks of New Caledonia*, Minority Rights Group International, London. 1986.

8 http://women.stormfront.org/Writings/notsink.html.

9 *Inquiries into Human Faculty and its Development*, Macmillan, London.

10 'Sweden to compensate sterilised women', BBC News Online. 4 March 1999.

11 Marek Kohn, *The Race Gallery*, Jonathan Cape, London. 1995.

P

1 Benno Muller-Hill, *Murderous Science: Elimination by Scientific Selection of Jews, Gypsies and Others, Germany 1933-1945*, Oxford University Press, Oxford. 1988.

2 These examples are taken from High Commissioner on National Minorities, Organisation for Security and Co-operation in Europe, *Report on the situation of Roma and Sinti in the OSCE Area*, The Hague, 2000.

3 Refugee Council, *Unwanted Journey*, London, 1999.

4 *Report on the situation of Roma and Sinti in the OSCE area*, op cit.

5 *Ibid.*

6 Refugee Council, *Unwanted Journey*, op cit.

7 *Report on the situation of the Roma and Sinti in the OSCE Area*, op cit.

8 *Concerns in Europe: July-December 1999*, AI Index: EUR 01/01/00.

9 Czech Helsinki Committee, *Annual Report* 1998, cited in Refugee Council, *Unwanted Journey*, op cit.

10 Kate Connolly, 'Gypsies trapped behind "European wall of shame"', *The Guardian*. 24 October 1999.

11 Refugee Council, *Unwanted Journey*, op cit.

Q

1 Graeme McLagan and Nick Lowles, *Mr Evil – The Secret Life of Racist Bomber and Killer David Copeland*, John Blake, London. 2000.

2 United States Holocaust Memorial Museum, 'Homosexuals: Victims of the Nazi Era', cited in Holocaust Teacher Resource Center, http://www.holocaust-trc.org/homosx.htm.

3 Thomas Robb, National Director, Knights of the Ku Klux Klan, http://www.kukluxklan.org/org/faq.htm.

4 *Ibid.*

5 Southern Poverty Law Center, http://www.splcenter.org/intelligenceproject/ip-4p2.html.

6 Martin E Marty, 'Oral Confession', *Christian Century*, 12/14/94, Volume 111 Issue 36.

R

1 Eldridge Cleaver, *Soul on Ice*, Jonathan Cape, London, 1969.

2 *Deuteronomy* 20:14.

3 Report to Commission on Human Rights, 26 January 1998 (E/CN.4/1998/54)

4 Susan Brownmiller, *Against Our Will: Men, Women and Rape*, Penguin, London. 1976.

5 *Report of the South African Truth and Reconciliation Commission*, Volume 4, Chapter 10.

6 'The situation of human rights in the territory of the former Yugoslavia – Note by the Secretary -General', A/48/92 S/25341, 26 February 1993.

7 George Schwarzenberger, *International Law as Applied by International Courts and Tribunals*, Volume II, *The Law of Armed Conflict*, Stevens and Sons Limited, London. 1968.

8 International Criminal Tribunal for Rwanda, The Prosecutor versus Jean-Paul Akayesu, Case Number ICTR-96-4-T, Decision of 2 September 1998.

9 International Criminal Tribunal for the former Yugoslavia, 'Celibici Case,' IT-96-21, Judgement 20 February 2001, Part IV.

S

1 Cited in Anthony Lewis, 'No Greater Tragedy', *The New York Times*, 24 March 2001.

2 Ian Hancock, *The Pariah Syndrome*, Karoma Publishers Inc, Michigan. 1987.

3 Linda Brent (Hariet Jacobs) *Incidents in the life of a slave girl – written by herself, Boston*, 1861.

4 'slavery', Encyclopaedia Britannica Online.

5 Eric Williams, *Capitalism and Slavery*, Capricorn Books, New York. 1996, cited in Dinesh D'Souza, *The End of Racism*, Free Press, 1996.

6 eg see Amnesty International, *Myanmar – Ethnic Minorities: Targets of Destruction*, AI Index 16/014/2001.

7 Kevin Bales, *Disposable People*, University of California Press, London. 1999.

8 US State Department www.state.gov/www/global/human_rights/1999_hrp_rep ort/overview.html. 6 July 2001.

9 Kevin Bales, *op cit.*

T

1 University of California Press, Berkeley, 1993.

2 *Ibid.*

3 This account of the case is based on Mertus, *ibid.*

4 *Ibid.*

5 *Ibid.*

6 Cecil Roth, *A Short History of the Jewish People*, East and West Library, London. 1959.

7 *Ibid.*

8 Reported in 'Anti-Semitic Blood Libel in Egypt's *al-Ahram*', Stephen Roth Institute for the Study of Anti-Semitism and Racism, Tel Aviv University, http://www.tau.ac.il/Anti-Semitism/updates/i00012.html. 6 July 2001.

9 'Tulsa Burning', Jonathan Z Larsen, *Civilization*. 1 February 1997.

10 *Ibid.*

U

1 4 March 1985.

2 'Sanctuary, Basic Rights and Humanity's Fault Lines', *Weber Studies*, Spring/Summer 1988, Volume 5.

3 In 'American Baptist Resolution on Church Sanctuary for Central American Refugees', adopted by the General Board of the American Baptist Churches. June 1985, modified September 1988. General Board Reference #8135:9/88.

4 US Department of State, *Human Rights Reports for 1999*, www.state.gov/www/global/human_rights/1999_hrp_repo rt/overview.html. 6 July 2001.

5 Jeremy Harding, *The Uninvited*, Profile Books, London. 2000.

6 Tim Sullivan and Raf Casert, 'In case we die', The Associated Press. 20 March 2000.

V

1 Reported in Human Rights Watch/Asia, *Burma – Entrenchment or Reform?* Volume 7, Number 10. 1995.

2 Minority Rights Group International, *World Directory of Minorities*, London. 1997.

3 Survival International, 'Botswana – "Bushmen" tortured for hunting', Urgent Action Bulletin. May 2001.

4 *The Star*, 19 June 1997, cited in communication from Survival International to the author.

5 CJ Chivers, 'From Court order to Reality: A Diverse Boston Police Force', *The New York Times*. 4 April 2001.

6 See for example, Bikhu Parekh, *Rethinking Multiculturalism*, Macmillan Press, London, 2000; Brian Barry, *Culture and Equality*, Polity Press, Cambridge, 2001; Kenan Malik, *The Meaning of Race*, Macmillan Press, London, 1996.

7 For example, see Jon Henley, 'I can't say to a wife of 20 years she has to go', *The Guardian*. 9 May 2001.

8 Johannes Morsink, 'Cultural Genocide, the Universal Declaration, and Minority Rights', *Human Rights Quarterly*, Volume 21, Number 4.

W

1 Henry Labouchere, *The Brown Man's Burden*, Literary Digest 18, 25 February 1899. Cited in Jim Zwick (ed), *Anti-Imperialism in the United States, 1898-1935*. http://www.boondocksnet.com/kipling/laboue.html.

2 *The Letters of Rudyard Kipling*, Volume 2, 1890-99, Macmillan, London. 1990.

3 The 'Laudabiliter' bull, a formal papal document, of 1155.

4 *L'Illustration*, November 1931. Cited in Arthur Chandler, 'Empire of the Republic: The Exposition Coloniale Internationale de Paris 1931', *World's Fair Magazine*, Volume VIII, Number 4, 1988.

5 The following account is based on Adam Hochschild, *King Leopold's Ghost*, Mariner Books, New York. 1999.

6 Leopold's welcoming speech to delegates to a conference that set up the International African Association, which became a vehicle to achieve his ambitions to secure a colony – cited in Adam Hochschild, op cit.

7 Sven Lindqvist, *Exterminate All The Brutes*, Granta, London, 1997.

8 'Britain and Europe', 20 September 1988. http://222.eurocritic.demon.co.uk/mtbruges.htm. 6 July 2001.

X

1 Edward Pearce, 'The Scum of Europe', *History Today*. November 2000.

2 *Collins Concise English Dictionary*, HarperCollins, Glasgow. 1992.

3 Robert Whymant, 'Japan faces its racism', *The Times*. 19 November 1999.

4 Andrea Mrozek, 'Foreigners and Fallout', *Central Europe Review*, Volume 29, Number 29. 4 September 2000.

5 Chris McGreal, '"Too black" migrants jailed in new South Africa', *The Guardian*. 18 November 2000.

6 Evidence Wa Ka Ngobeni, 'Go home, foreigners', *Mail & Guardian*. 14 September 1998.

7 *European Race Bulletin*, Numbers 32, 33, 34, Institute of Race Relations, London. 2000.

8 Cian McCormack and Sarah Murphy, 'Cead mile failte for refugees as accommodation rooms gutted', *Irish Examiner*. 26 April 2000.

9 Tom Stacey, *Immigration and Enoch Powell*, Tom Stacey Ltd, London. 1970.

10 'Diary on Irish Racism', 19 June 2000. sites.netscape.net/rarireland/racist_diary. 21 August 2000.

11 Robert Shepherd, *Enoch Powell – A Biography*, Hutchinson, London. 1996.

12 Nicholas Fraser, *The Voice of Modern Hatred*, Picador, London. 2000.

13 *Dover Express*. 1 October, 1998.

14 Association of Chief Police Officers, *ACPO Guide to Meeting the Policing needs of Asylum Seekers and Refugees*, UK. 2001.

15 *Austria before the UN Committee against Torture*, AI Index: EUR 13/01/00.

Y

1 *The Golden Era*, 26 July 1901, British Columbia, Canada. http://www.fortsteele.bc.ca.

2 Anthony Howard ed., *The Crossman Diaries*, Magnum Books, London. 1979.

Z

1 http://www.bloodandhonour.com/cheight.htm. 6 July 2001.

2 http://www.heretical.co.uk/bhengland/zog.html. 6 July 2001.

3 See, for example, The Jewish Student Online Research Center, *The Protocols of the Elders of Zion*, www.us-israel.org/jsource/anti-semitism/protocols.html.

4 Adolf Hitler, *Mein Kampf*, Reynal and Hitchcock, New York. 1939.

5 David Segal, 'The Pied Piper of Racism: William Pierce Wants Young People to March to his Hate Records', *Washington Post*. 12 January 2000.

6 Kate Taylor ed., *Holocaust Denial*, Searchlight Educational Trust, London. 2000.

7 *The Irving Judgment*, Penguin, London. 2000.

Amnesty International's mandate is to promote the values of the Universal Declaration of Human Rights and to work worldwide for the release of prisoners of conscience, fair trials for political prisoners and an end to torture, extra-judicial executions, 'disappearances' and the death penalty.

● ● ●

For more information and details of membership contact:

Amnesty International United Kingdom
99-119 Rosebery Avenue, London EC1R 4RE
Tel: 020 7814 6200 Fax: 020 7833 1510
Website: http://www.amnesty.org.uk/